Adirondack Voices celebrates the storytelling and folksong traditions of men who have spent much of their lives in the "Big Woods" of the western Adirondack foothills. Writing for the general reader as well as the specialist, Bethke takes great care to relate these "folk" to their native "lore," to portray faithfully the people who embody and give voice to their oral traditions.

The stories, reminiscences, and songs recorded by Bethke reflect the woodsmen's love for the spoken word and help recover a legacy of work, recreation, talk, and singing associated with an earlier lumbering era. He devotes one chapter to a colorful innkeeper/raconteur and his captivating tales. Two other chapters examine the personalities and folksinging talents of two brothers who spent nearly forty years working in the lumberwoods, composing songs, and entertaining peers in bunkhouses, barrooms, and homes. Additional chapters focus on other local woods singers, the native folksongs and their antecedents, and the range of stories and oral history associated with the region. Based upon fieldwork conducted between 1970 and 1977 in New York State's largest county (St. Lawrence), Bethke's is the first book-length study of New York folklife and oral traditions to deal exclusively with woodsmen and lumbering.

"This is a good picture of lumbercamp storytelling and singing as it was and, to some extent, still is in the Adirondacks. Bob Bethke looked — and listened — hard and what he came up with is well worth any folklorist's attention." — Edward D. Ives, author of

Additional volumes on the folklore of working men from the series **Music in American Life**

Adirondack Voices

Robert D. Bethke

Adirondack Voices

Woodsmen and Woods Lore

UNIVERSITY OF ILLINOIS PRESS

Urbana · Chicago · London

*Publication of this book was supported in part by a grant from the
University of Delaware.*

© 1981 by the Board of Trustees of the University of Illinois
Manufactured in the United States of America

For permission to reprint copyrighted material, the author is indebted to the California Folklore Society, for portions of his essay
"Storytelling at an Adirondack Inn," *Western Folklore*, 35 (1976),
123–39.

Library of Congress Cataloging in Publication Data

Bethke, Robert D   1945–
    Adirondack voices.

    Includes index.
    1. Logging (in religion, folklore, etc.)—New York
(State)—Adirondack Mountain region.   2. Adirondack
Mountain region, N.Y.—Social life and customs.
3. Loggers—New York (State)—Adirondack Mountain
region—Songs and music—History and criticism.
4. Folk-Songs, American—New York (State)—Adirondack
Mountain region—History and criticism.   5. Folk-lore—
New York (State)—Adirondack Mountain region.
I. Title.
GR110.N7B47   398'.09747'56   80-24054
ISBN 0-252-00829-4

To Barbara, Peter, and Tina

And to many voices from
the Adirondack woods,
some of them now silent.
The echoes live in endur-
ing memories.

Contents

Preface   ix

1   Woods at the Doorstep   3

2   "Get to the Bush!"   11

3   Bunkhouse Yarns   25

4   Big Woods, "Big Stories"   38

5   Lumbering and Foothills Folksong Tradition   55

6   The Roving Ashlaw Man   80

7   Ted Ashlaw, Solitary Singer   99

8   Beyond Sunday Rock   139

Index   143

Stories are things if you don't tell them right along, you forget 'em. Only time I'll tell one now is if somebody tells one. Then it will kind of remind me of one similar to it. . . .

In the woods there were some pretty good singers. Years ago you sang a lot. If you were in bars, you sang. Today you don't. It's a different class of people.

EDDIE ASHLAW
Parishville, New York
1970, 1972

Preface

This book is about workingmen and shared folk tradition in northern New York State. It is about a recoverable past, one recoverable through the storytelling and folksong heritages, the recollected experiences, and the personalities of elderly woodsmen. I focus upon the western Adirondack foothills, an area off the beaten path. The region is better known for its tourist lure than its grassroots lore. The study results from my folklore fieldwork conducted between 1970 and 1977 in central and eastern St. Lawrence County, the largest county (2,767 square miles) in the state.

Easygoing talk and venerable yarns mingle freely among Adirondack woodsmen. Anyone on familiar terms with North Country hunting camps or backroad taverns knows that. But many people lack such exposure. There is a popular image of Yankee-stock outdoorsmen as a taciturn breed not given much to talk, particularly with strangers. The so-called laconic Yankee rustic is a familiar stereotype: elderly, reticent, and wary of city folks or academic types who intrude upon his native soil and lifestyle. Such, at any rate, is the image frequently projected through American regional writing, popular drama, cartoons, jests, and the like. I trust that the evidence of my account will serve in part to counteract such blanket impressions, at least for Northern New York.

In the storytelling portion of the book I present a series of elderly woodsmen who enjoy talk and talking—especially when that medium relates to immediate personal and regional experience. They are not unique. Indeed, my findings indicate that many Adirondack woodsmen are highly expressive individuals with equally expressive stories about their work and recreation in the outdoors. Their yarns resonate with collective experience, as do the men themselves. To be sure, some woodsmen are less inclined to verbalize than others. It's as much that way in Northern New York as it is in neighboring Vermont, or in Maine. But there are also plenty of talkers. The majority of North Country men whom I met or heard about have valued the spoken word. Their fraternizing among peers is talk filled. And their talk ranges from introspective reminiscence and personal opinion to entertaining, well-traveled yarns. In short, my inquiries often prompted stories that under other circumstances are a natural and indelible part of native woodsmen lifestyle, a pattern not exclusive to the North Country.

Whereas traditions of oral prose narrative continue to flourish among western Adirondack woodsmen, the folksong heritage of former lumbermen among them is today much less in evidence. "Woods singers" and "woods singing" represent an earlier era. For that reason alone there is an urgent need to document the musical heritage from the perspective of elderly men who participated in it firsthand. Heretofore, no such study had been undertaken in the portion of New York State of which I write.

Collections abound containing folksongs obtained from American lumbermen. Several excellent ones concentrate on the Northeast and neighboring Canada, and I refer to them in my notes. Often, however, the accounts have spotlighted songs at the expense of singers. One is left with the impression that traditional song texts and tunes are somehow more important, more worth documenting, than the kinds of individuals and activities and attitudes behind them. Part of my aim is to restore the human element without sacrificing the expressive materials. Although songs sometimes outlive men, some men outlive the currency of certain songs. In the case of folk tradition it seems mistaken to pay tribute to only half of the relationship. Throughout the volume I stress the fusion of past and present lore with persons, places, and folk performances.

I am often asked what I do as a folklorist—a legitimate question to pose to someone in professional academic life. Generally I reply that my work has included some extremely rewarding field experiences in the Adirondacks. The conversation inevitably turns to some of the details. I offer anecdotes and fragmentary vignettes, I share impressions. So much is left unsaid. Colleagues at the University of Delaware, where I teach, have heard that I have spent a good deal of time interviewing and recording in rural parlors and rustic barrooms. They frequently smile when the matter comes up, and we make jokes. A few professors on my English Department faculty are openly skeptical. Doing serious research in a kitchen or tavern isn't exactly like pondering elusive literary passages. Well, they're right.

In a secondary way this book is about the nature of my fieldwork experience. I see no rationale for hiding behind a pseudo-objective voice or point of view. Folklore fieldwork requires substantial personal involvement and, inevitably, subjective filtering of what one learns and perceives in the role. Similarly, the images conveyed through the words of field contacts reflect how they as participant-observers have filtered personal and shared experiences, emotions, and impressions. I have attempted to align the various perspectives. The result, I hope, approximates an "insider's" vision, a valid portrayal recognizable among the men who informed me. That goal cautions against overinterpretations and imposed analytical frameworks. I am willing to err on the side of sympathetic, humanistic description. In many ways, the men and the lore best tell their own stories.

Adirondack woodsmen deserve to be heard the way they actually talk. Excerpts from my field tapes are quoted verbatim, although here and there edited for continuity. I have also eliminated the redundancies of natural speech. Self-contained oral narratives, however, are transcribed unaltered from field-recorded performances, as are song texts and tunes. I am grateful to Norman Cazden for tackling the musical transcription with his recognized expertise and careful attention to vocal nuance. He also assisted in the annotations.

I have avoided using pseudonyms for field contacts and persons to whom they refer. I assume full responsibility if this procedure causes unintentional embarrassment of any sort. The several storytellers and singers whom I feature became aware over time that I intended to publish my findings. They expected me to be accurate and judicious in reporting what I learned, and I have strived to meet that expectation. Some of my elderly contacts have not lived to see this work into print. Others, or relatives, may wish that I had not identified certain individuals or circumstances. Let it be said that I have done my best to present the woodsmen, as their storytelling and song heritages, with respect and admiration.

Using a 35 mm camera, I took more than a thousand still photographs over the duration of the field experience. From that number I have selected a small sample of images to help provide a visual context for the written account. For permission to include several historical photos I am grateful to the Adirondack Museum, Blue Mountain Lake. Unless otherwise indicated, all photographs are from my collection.

I am indebted to many people for help and encouragement at all stages of this project. A University of Pennsylvania Predoctoral Fellowship provided support during the early phase of my fieldwork. A University of

Delaware faculty research grant and sabbatical leave facilitated continued research and completion of the manuscript. My wife, Barbara, watched the inquiry unfold from the beginning and cheerfully tolerated my jumble of field equipment, phone calls, hasty explanations, and hours away from family and friends. Sensitive to the ups and downs of such work, she helped me recognize what needed to be said. Judith McCulloh at the University of Illinois Press made gracious suggestions on how best to say it. Others who deserve special thanks include colleagues Roger Abrahams, Richard Bauman, James Curtis, William Ferris, Edith Fowke, Henry Glassie, Kenneth Goldstein, and Edward "Sandy" Ives, all good friends and perceptive critics. At the Adirondack Museum, Blue Mountain Lake, I benefited from research and editorial help provided by Craig and Alice Gilborn, William Verner, the late Marcia Smith, and other members of the staff. St. Lawrence County historian Mary Biondi Smallman and many other residents guided me to useful background materials, as did Marion Brophy and Marion C. Thompson at the Harold W. Thompson Folklore Archive, New York State Historical Association, Cooperstown. Nancy Bixler, assistant director of the North Country Research Center, St. Lawrence University, arranged and recorded a storytelling session with Ham Ferry that I moderated on that campus in April, 1977. She gave permission to use material from the tape. Finally, I owe a special debt to a dozen or so North Country acquaintances who provided entree and volunteered invaluable leads of all sorts. While their names may not appear in this book, I am confident they will recognize their contribution between the lines.

I reserve a separate paragraph for the woodsmen and members of their families. It is impossible to thank each of them adequately. I came to them as a stranger less than half their age; largely because of them, I now feel more at home in their native surroundings.

Adirondack
Voices

1

Woods at the Doorstep

"When I was a kid this was all virgin forest, from here in Colton clear up through Tupper Lake," Otis Schofell recalled as he settled back in a Victorian armchair and gazed through the dusty windowpane. "There was nothin' but a dirt road up through there." It was the summer of 1970, and I had traveled to the Adirondack foothills of St. Lawrence County to meet men like Otis. We talked over a cup of coffee poured from a tarnished metal thermos. His shack was on property within earshot of a modern public school. I could imagine the sound of children's voices at recess during the school year. How many of them had wandered down the hill to hear his stories? Probably very few, and there was little time left. Several logging trucks rumbled past us, heading northward on Route 56 toward Potsdam. The shack shuddered a little as if in protest.

Otis continued. Ninety-one years old, he had witnessed a lot of changes during his lifetime. He told of his boyhood fishing trips to backwoods tributaries of the neighboring Raquette River; of the winter fifty years earlier when he made barrels and worked in the lumber woods for the Brooklyn Cooperage Company, at forty-five dollars a month plus room and board; and of the times he scaled timber and kept books for local firms like the Oval Wood Dish Company and St. Regis Paper Company. He went on, filling my tape recorder with "yarns" (his term) about the "good old days, gone forever." Otis was an Adirondack woodsman who liked to talk.

Otis Schofell died the following January after a short illness. He lies at rest in Pleasant Mound Cemetery. His shack eventually burned to the ground; the property is now well-cut grass.

Like his rustic dwelling, Otis was in many ways an anachronism. He was, by general acclaim, the most colorful character in town, Colton's oldest living resident. Charlie Berry, who lived a mile or so down the road, went out of his way to introduce us. I was forewarned that Otis had grown hard of hearing and was given to lengthy, disjointed reminiscence. Some said that he was too senile to take very seriously, especially on matters of oral history. The portrayal scarcely did justice to the man and the past he represented. I think most of the townspeople knew that. One-time lumberman, railroad worker, blacksmith, farmer, and local volunteer fireman, Otis was a man and voice out of an earlier generation. He looked the part in his well-worn plaid shirt and rumpled dark trousers. Otis was at home in the woods at his doorstep. And in his own way he was eloquent when he talked about the environment and experiences he knew best.

I used to go into the woods years ago with an old-timer by the name of Deacon Butler. He run a store here back in the Civil War days. And after the war was over there was him and an old-time fellow by the name of Jock Maldrin. They went together and built themselves a nice log cabin up to Moosehead in back of Sevey's there, at the foot of Moosehead Stillwater. And he used to invite me to go up to that camp and stay with him there a month or so in the fall, along September and October, back when I was a youngster.

Well, when we were going up through there, we used to take a boat and row up the river. And there was a big flat rock at the foot of an island. And it was kinda swift water. And as we were going by there one day he pointed out to me and said, "Old Harv Averill and I used to pull our boat up on that rock right there, and we would set and catch a sixty-weight tub full of trout without ever moving."

He said he wasn't much of a hunter himself—said the most deer he ever killed in the woods in the fall was thirty-two. But old Mat Daniel, he killed some ninety-odd, and Uncle Eben Willis, who lived as a next-door neighbor to me, he killed a hundred and ten in the course of one hunting season.

Fish and game are more elusive nowadays in the foothills, but the lure of the woods among men like Otis Schofell continues. Glenn Spear is a case in point. His name came up one evening as I sat drinking beer at Elroy Sochia's Cedar Lodge, near Parishville. Local regulars know it better, more personally, as "Elroy's place." The tavern provides surroundings as good as any in the foothills, if one wishes to meet and hear about woodsmen on their own terms. Elroy is one of those woodsmen. He and

Otis Schofell, woodsman, at his home in Colton, N.Y., June, 1970.

his wife say they try to run a "nice friendly place catering to the older crowd." No one familiar with it would disagree. Those who respond to the woods feel at home, among family, at Elroy's establishment. Elroy suggested that I might pay Glenn a visit. They had cut wood and hunted together.

There was no problem finding the house. The mounted buck deer head with the impressive antlers hung beside the front door, as Elroy had said. He hadn't told me that Glenn was pretty much homebound, battling advanced cancer. It wasn't something one talked about with strangers. Besides, Glenn could speak for himself. We sat down next to a majestic wood-burning parlor stove, and at seventy-four Glenn reflected on some of the things that had made his years special.

I worked on the town road and for the state, between Potsdam and Massena, for nine years. In between, when I wasn't doing that, I cut wood. I cut wood for a living. I draw a small Social Security check. But cuttin' wood, I can

Cedar Lodge, near Parishville, N.Y., June, 1976.

keep going and I manage all right. I love to cut wood. Oh boy, if I could get out in the woods today and cut wood I'd be the happiest man in the world. I sure would.

There's a man who just bought some wood off me. Art Mann, his name is. Had a camp up in the woods. We used to go up in the woods there in the wintertime and cut wood. Another fella and I. When it come noon, we'd go over to this camp and build a fire and eat our dinner in there.

Well, this time I went up in there huntin'. I was all alone. I was only about eighteen years old, I guess. I had a twenty-gauge shotgun. A single-shot. Well, I see this deer down in the valley in front of me, and I shot. I hit the deer, but it didn't kill it right there; it run away for at least half a mile. But I could track it by the blood, and when I come to that deer it lay right back of a great big log. And it looked right at me and it said, "Baaaa." Just like that. My God, it took the heart right out of me. It was a long time I couldn't shoot another deer—but I finally got over it!

I used to guide the boys all up in these woods because I knew every runway [i.e., deer trail]. The boys used to say they could drop me right out of an airplane and I'd come out of the woods all right, because I'd never get lost. I've been in the woods all my life and I don't worry at all about getting lost.

To listen to elderly woodsmen like Otis and Glenn is to gain a sense of their lifelong intimacy with the outdoors. In the timbered foothills of eastern St. Lawrence County it could hardly be otherwise. Communities there are scattered and rarely exceed two thousand persons. In general, their populations are on the decline. Modern single-family mobile homes have begun to replace many of the older and modest frame dwellings. Currently, the economy is stagnant and depressed, although subject to some seasonal and annual fluctuation. What hasn't changed much is the woods. It was there when early nineteenth-century Yankee families came from places like Vermont and New Hampshire. It was there when mid-century Irish and French-Canadian settlers joined them, crossing the international border that separates Northern New York from eastern Ontario and the Eastern Townships of Quebec. And the woods is there at present, continuing to isolate the foothills region from the more prosperous St. Lawrence Valley dairy farm country to the west. In all, the presence of the woods shapes the tenor of foothills work, recreation, and talk. Wrote seasoned woodsman Herbert F. Keith in *Man of the Woods*, "Compared to the northwestern half of St. Lawrence County, our southeastern half is definitely backwoods. That is holstein country, sloping down to the St. Lawrence. This is whitetail, beaver, and tall pine country. We don't pretend to be as civilized as our neighbors on the north, who used to turn the tables on city people downstate by calling our part of the county the South Woods and claiming it as their playground."

Foothills woodsmen as a group are cognizant of this qualitative difference. Ask them about it in the environs of South Colton and one is very apt to hear about Sunday Rock, which rests alongside Route 56 just north of town. As Charlie Berry put it, the huge glacial boulder is nothing less than the equivalent of the "local Plymouth Rock," for "in the old days, life took on a different character beyond that rock: there were no ministers, no schools." Residents tell how it once stood in the middle of the thoroughfare, forcing buggies to pass to one side. With the introduction of automobiles, highway department officials decided in 1925 that the road needed straightening. They prepared to dynamite Sunday Rock. Local residents had other ideas. To their way of thinking, Sunday Rock was no ordinary obstacle. Incensed townspeople formed a Sunday Rock Association and raised sufficient funds to have the boulder moved to one side, where it remained for forty years. In 1965 it was shifted once again during road improvements. But this time there was no longer any doubt that it deserved preservation as a foothills landmark. Today, Sunday Rock rests in permanent symbolic testimony to a lifestyle

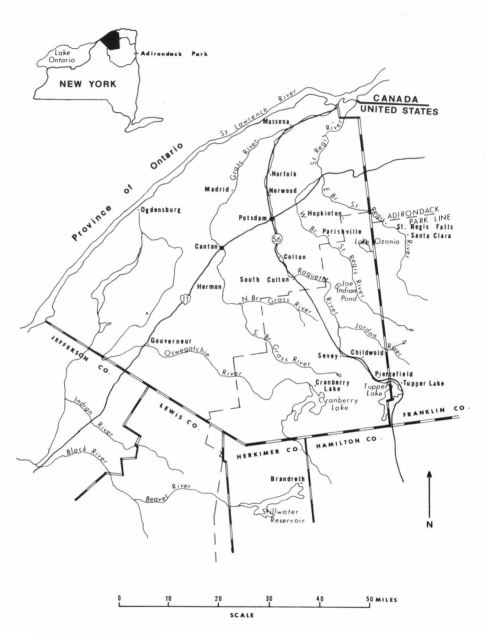

ST. LAWRENCE COUNTY, NEW YORK
Source: U.S.G.S. Topographic Map, New York Series

Cartography by Susan Marshall

Sunday Rock at South Colton, N.Y., July, 1970.

as it has developed beyond the valley. Historically, those patterns have emerged largely as a consequence of male-dominated activities: lumbering, hunting and fishing, and camaraderie enhanced through social drinking and in-group talk. The foundation is deep rooted and enduring.

Tourists come and go in the Adirondacks. For them the woods is a temporary refuge, a sanctuary, an idyll. For native woodsmen the forest is an everyday presence. The big timber expanse beyond Sunday Rock means more to them than relative freedom to do as they please. That is definitely part of the lure. But in my experience few area woodsmen speak of the domain in pastoral terms. They know that one can love the woods without glossing over its reality.

It is a mistake, then, to view the woodsmen heard in these pages as misty-eyed backwoods romantics. In truth they have been independent, practical-minded, hardworking men. Many of them have known hardship in one form or another. Yet in retrospect they have enjoyed their heritage of woods work and recreation, and they take pleasure in celebrating it in the present. The stories they tell represent real-life experience (and what is meant to pass for it) selected, organized, manipulated, and projected. Each oral history account, each yarn recollected amounts to a photograph retrieved for new viewing from the archive of memory. The same holds for "the old songs that one doesn't hear no more." Collectively, these photographs-in-words convey much of what it has meant to be a woodsman during the past half-century or so in the western Adirondack foothills. One has but to listen.

Notes

The notes following each chapter include pertinent bibliographic citations, brief annotations for tales and songs, and suggested supplementary readings and recordings. My aim has been to be indicative rather than exhaustive; whenever possible, I have cited key secondary sources in which the reader will find more extensive annotations and commentary.

Excellent historical and pictorial treatments of northern New York State, and in particular the Adirondacks, are available through Syracuse University Press and the Adirondack Museum, Blue Mountain Lake. Personal recollections, illustrated historical sketches, and essays on St. Lawrence Valley folklife appear regularly in the *Quarterly* (Canton, N.Y.: St. Lawrence County Historical Association, 1955 –). For a grassroots sense of St. Lawrence County, see also Luther H. Gulick, Jr., Charles Lahey, and Carleton Mabee, *The St. Lawrence Valley: Avenue of History* (Gouverneur, N.Y.: St. Lawrence Valley Association, 1964), and Edith L. Costa and Mary H. Biondi, *Top o' the State* (Ogdensburg, N.Y.: Northern New York Publishing Co., 1967). On the western foothills sector see Charles W. Bryan, Jr., *The Raquette: River of the Forest* (Blue Mountain Lake, N.Y.: Adirondack Museum, 1964); Lorena Bullis Reed et al., *Colton: Story of a Town* (Colton, N.Y., 1976); Roy C. Higby, . . . *A Man from the Past*, ed. Ray Hanlon (Big Moose, N.Y.: Big Moose Press, 1974); and Herbert F. Keith, *Man of the Woods*, with introduction and notes by Paul F. Jamieson (Syracuse: Syracuse University Press, Adirondack Museum Books, 1972). The Keith quotation is from p. 139. The latter two works are reminiscences of foothills woodsmen and as such have special relevance. Reed et al., *Colton*, pp. 73–75, summarizes the fate of Sunday Rock.

For background on North Country oral tradition, one should consult Harold W. Thompson, *Body, Boots & Britches: Folktales, Ballads and Speech from Country New York* (1939; rpt., New York: Dover Publications, 1962), and Edith E. Cutting, *Lore of an Adirondack County* (1944; rpt., Elizabethtown, N.Y.: Denton Publications, 1972). Both are scholarly works addressed to the general reader. Note also the special issue "The Adirondacks," *New York Folklore Quarterly*, 22:2 (June, 1966). There are various other collections of Northern New York lore in print, but most contain rewritten oral texts and spotty information on the collecting circumstances and materials. Examples from the southern tier include Howard Thomas, *Tales from the Adirondack Foothills* (Prospect, N.Y.: Prospect Books, 1956), and his follow-up *Folklore from the Adirondack Foothills* (Prospect, N.Y.: Prospect Books, 1958); and from the northern tier, Helen Escha Tyler, *Log Cabin Days: Folk Tales of the Adirondacks* (Saranac Lake, N.Y.: Currier Press, 1969).

Since 1977, major efforts have been made by the Center for the Study of North Country Folklife to document, preserve, and present all aspects of North Country folklife. An inaugural survey of St. Lawrence County concentrated on material folk culture and traditional instrumental music. The center and its archives are located at the State University of New York Agricultural and Technical College, Canton, N.Y. 13617.

2

"Get to the Bush!"

"**M**ighty *Jesus, get to the bush!*" was a cry with which Parishville logging foreman Hadie Brown once aroused his woods crew. It is no longer heard in the western foothills. Hadie has been dead for years. The sleep-in lumbercamps are, with minor exceptions, a thing of the past. But memories of the camps endure, and local personalities like Hadie Brown are not easily forgotten. Nor are accounts that express the occupational workers' strong sense of their experience.

"Back in the late nineties or early 1900s," seventy-six-year-old Fay Duffy recalled one afternoon,

> there weren't automobiles around. They had these traveler sleighs, two-seated. And they were lumbering in the woods up here in Parishville. Repairing the roadway by hauling up logs. It was a transition road—they'd cut smaller logs and put them in, and then throw water on it. It would freeze overnight. So these fellas were fixin' up the road. They called them "road monkeys" in those days. And they tell that story about Mrs. Simeon Clark going up there with her daughter-in-law and her husband [S. L. Clark and Son Co. was a prominent Parishville lumbering firm].
>
> So Mrs. Clark was driving along and said, "What are those men there?"
>
> "Why," he says, "those are road monkeys."
>
> "Why," she says, "they look just like human beings!"

Fay Duffy heard that story one day in his Parishville barbershop. Said Fay, "A lot of things come back to you, you know, after you get to reminiscing. Fellas are talking and stories come up. I used to hear some good stories in the barbershop." And well he might, for among former loggers there are plenty of experiences to talk about. Take the chronicle of the

11

rise, change, and eventual decline of large-scale lumbering in and around eastern St. Lawrence County. It remains a significant aspect of the area's social history. But it is not history confined to the printed page. Ask any woodsman or listen to the talk when men congregate at spots like Remington's garage, down the street from Duffy's barbershop. For it is in those surroundings, rather than in the halls of nearby SUNY-Potsdam, that the historians of the woods regularly gather. They are the unselfconscious oral historians whose credentials attest to firsthand participation in their own lumbering heritage. To know that heritage is to know them better in the present.

Evidence of lumbering in Northern New York dates to the mid-eighteenth century. French-Canadian loggers cut timber near the mouths of the Raquette and Oswegatchie rivers for transportation by raft down the St. Lawrence River to Montreal. During the period from 1790 to 1850 the state gradually surpassed New England in pre-eminence as the leading region for lumber production in the Northeast. The most extensive operations developed in the eastern Adirondacks at the headwaters of the Hudson River. Glens Falls, in particular, achieved prominence as a lumbering center; its reputation rivaled that of Bangor, Maine. Towns on the opposite side of the Adirondack divide also responded to the economic incentive, but most of their mills were small in comparison to standards set to the east.

Adirondack lumbering prior to the conclusion of the Civil War relied heavily upon virgin timber: white pine, spruce, and hemlock. The re-

Lumbercamp crew, near Parishville, N.Y., about 1900. Photograph courtesy of Mr. and Mrs. Frank Daniels.

Adirondack lumbercamp in the Big Woods setting, about 1900. Photograph courtesy of the Adirondack Museum.

source was depleted rapidly. As it dwindled, the center of the cutting activities moved progressively toward Northern New York's interior. By the 1890s, lumber companies operating around Tupper Lake had turned increasingly to second- and third-growth softwood. Nature simply could not keep pace with the heavy timber harvests. Adoption of a "forever wild" statute applicable to State Forest Preserve lands and formation of the Adirondack Park placed new restrictions on long-log cutting. Severe wind and ice storms created additional problems, as did a series of devastating forest fires between 1903 and 1908. The latter were attributed in part to coal-burning railroad locomotives in the service of loggers. This combination of factors together with new demands for paper stimulated the rise of the pulpwood industry in the western foothills. The industry was well under way by 1910, roughly the point at which recollections begin among the oldest ex-loggers in the foothills.

Foothills logging in the years preceding World War I depended wholly upon manual labor to cut the timber, and upon men, horses, and rivers to move it. By and large, women and children were considered ill suited for the physically taxing work routine and out of their element in the male-oriented environment. Exceptions were made for women cooks and their offspring, and in instances when a crew boss wished to bring his family into the woods. Some men devoted full time to the profession. Others, especially farmers and itinerants, preferred to work seasonally.

Santa Clara Lumber Company camp and crew. Photograph courtesy of the Adirondack Museum.

Ted Ashlaw of Hermon told me a great deal about these kinds of things. Ted spent some thirty years cutting and hauling pulp for various outfits. He was born in 1905 at lumbercamp "No. 1" operated by the St. Regis Paper Company. The camp was near the town of Santa Clara, located in neighboring Franklin County. His father, a farmer, worked off and on as a teamster for the firm. His mother served for a time as the camp's cook. Disabled in a log-loading accident in 1947, Ted now lives in relative solitude. His thoughts often return to his past.

Ted recalls that in the early years the mature, married wage earners formed the backbone of most crews. "Back when I was kid, there wasn't too many young fellas who worked in the woods. I don't know why. And when they started to come in, the younger fellas, most of 'em didn't stay any length of time. They'd work a week and get. The only ones that would stay and work, when you'd stay in camp, were the men with families, the married men. The young fellas, if they did come in, you'd see them this week but you wouldn't see them the next."

Crews ranged from about fifteen to eighty or more men, the number varying with the nature of the operation. While some deep-woods camps were accessible by train, the majority were isolated and difficult to reach. Eddie Ashlaw, Ted's seventy-six-year-old brother who lives near Parishville, remembers walking twenty-eight miles into the wilderness to reach a camp near McKeever. "You had to dodge the mudholes," he told me during one of our many talks, "or they toted you with wagons. You couldn't walk the road half the time. You didn't come out every night! This buddy of mine, Herb McGhee, he'd been in there a year and a half. A lot of 'em had been in there two years, hadn't been out of camp."

Santa Clara woods crew at a skidway in the days of long logs and torchlight. Photograph courtesy of the Adirondack Museum.

A work cycle that varied with wood types and the seasons dictated the daily routine. Softwood sawlogs were cut and "skid" by horse teams to loading sites during the fall and early winter. Pulp was cut and hemlock peeled during the summer, beginning in late May. In either case, in late winter, teamsters hauled the logs along iced roads to rivers or railroad cars. Come spring, rivermen "drove" the softwood down major rivers to mills for commercial processing. Hardwood cutting was more sporadic; because hardwood logs floated poorly, harvesting and transporting them became commonplace only after the advent of truck hauling.

An Adirondack logger's working hours were long and strenuous. Ted Ashlaw knows from experience:

> One winter I worked in back of Piercefield for Leo McCarthy. That was sup-posed to be a one-trip haul, and he made two. We used to have breakfast about one in the morning. The teamsters would get up about midnight to feed their horses. We'd go out and load logs soon after 1:00 A.M. and get our round loaded by about 5:00 A.M., with three or four gangs of loaders. Then we'd haul. We'd be back in camp, eat again, and go in the bunkhouse. Maybe raise hell for a little while, or maybe go to bed about 9:00 or 9:30. Then the first teams would start coming back. As soon as the horses were fed, they'd get you up. And that started another round. 'Course, a lot of times we were loading the sonofabitchin' logs at nine or ten o'clock at night, too, with them old kero-sene torches.
>
> We didn't get much money in the woods in those days. We'd be in there with lanterns in the morning and were in there with lanterns at night. I think loading we got seventy cents a day—fifty cents if you were cutting.

Winter hauling in the western foothills. Note the sprinkler wagon used for icing the tote road. Photograph courtesy of Edward Ashlaw.

The nature of the work required construction of lumbercamps from rough-hewn logs, boards, bark, and tarpaper. An average camp consisted of a bunkhouse, eating and cooking quarters, and various outbuildings for horses and equipment. The close living quarters had drawbacks.

One hazard was the continual nuisance of bedbugs and human body lice. Men alternately cursed them and made sport of their presence. There was need to relieve the very real anxieties occasioned by the pests. Indeed, loggers were inclined to evaluate operations and individual camps largely in terms of the annoyance. I well recall asking Eddie Ashlaw about bunkhouse bedbugs and lice. His response was frank, graphic, and spiced with suitable hyperbole. "We were cuttin' wood for the Newton Brothers at Raquette Lake," he began, his voice intense at the recollection. "The goddamn bedbugs were so thick on the bunks they were hung all on haywires, each of the four corners of the bed. And still they'd run the ceiling and jump on you, them friggin' body lice as big as that." He gestured to indicate the size of his thumbnail. "Some guys would be in the top of the bunk. They'd pick 'em off and throw 'em on the other guy. They'd pet 'em awhile. Why, shit, there's no need trying to get rid of them—too many! But the lousiest camp was Bush LaPorte's, and one camp near Piercefield that Leo McCarthy run. I never seen the lice so big!"

Hamilton "Ham" Ferry of Childwold had similar exposure in the 1920s. He likes to tell about working one winter at a camp on Little Blue

Mountain. "That was a rough winter. Oh, boy, it was cold that winter. They said it was so cold that the thermometer went about a cardboard below the thermometer." And there were lice, "the biggest lice I ever seen in my life. Honest to Jesus, they were almost as big as my little fingernail. Body lice. I was plastered with the goddamn lice."

Predictably, yarns arose about men who were worse off. Ham tells a beauty, often to wrap up his personal experience. I've heard local men challenge the authenticity of its specifics but never once the truth at its core.

> Well, this guy comes in from the lumber woods and stops in to Bill Clark's. Clark used to run the gun store in Colton. And he says, "Hi, Bill." (He was very low-spoken.)
>
> He says, "Hi, Joe. Where have you been?"
>
> "I've been working in a lumbercamp."
>
> "Working in a lumbercamp? How are you doing?"
>
> He says, "All right."
>
> He says, "What do you want?"
>
> He says, "I want to buy some anguinum."
>
> He says, "How much do you want?"
>
> He says, "About ten pounds."
>
> "What are you going to do with ten pounds of anguinum?"
>
> He says, "I'm going to kill lice."
>
> "Ohhh," Bill says, "that could kill all the lice in St. Lawrence County."
>
> He says, "Bill, I've *got* them!"

Bunkhouse living quarters. In addition to the bedbugs and lice, "the place smelled of a good many pairs of socks." Photograph courtesy of the Adirondack Museum.

Few jobs in the Adirondack lumber woods earned a man more respect than that of river-driver. To be a "white-water man," to use Eddie Ashlaw's terminology, was to be among the elite. River-driving was specialized enough to require a separate crew and foreman. Accomplishment as a river-driver demanded considerable agility and stamina, and many of the best were wiry French-Canadians and Irishmen of short stature. Eddie weighed between 160 and 165 pounds as a young man and fit the physical requirements. He speaks with awe of his river-driving in the 1920s. "I drove six or seven springs," he told me. "That was a sonofabitchin' stream, that Moose River. Wide, and she's fast and rough when that water is high and all the rivers come into it. You'd see a little white water there! That was something I wouldn't want to do again. Boy, that's a hard business. Rough work."

Ted Ashlaw was very willing to leave river-driving to individuals like his older brother, especially when the drive involved pulp. Working pulp, a man expected to get wet; there was little of the glamour of hopping and riding the long logs.

> A river-drive, I think, they never stopped. They worked seven days. Once they got that going they kept right at it. They pretty near had to or they would have lost a lot of time. And some of them river-drives, you know, went a long ways.

River-drivers working "dead water." Photograph courtesy of the Adirondack Museum.

I went up one time on a river-drive for the St. Regis Paper Company and I guess I worked a day and a half, two days at the most. And I quit that. The hell with that! Anybody that liked it, it was all right. There was always somebody there with a basket full of stuff to eat and hot coffee or tea. Or whatever you wanted. But, Jesus, you'd get out sometimes in the morning and there was several inches of ice on there. And you had to wade into that water to push that pulp out of them coves. I said the hell with that—I didn't go for that stuff!

But not everyone shared Ted's view. Irishman Ned Long, who came to South Colton from County Cork at the age of seven, was the kind of man who welcomed the drives. He was eighty-nine when I located him in the fall of 1975, two years before his death. Ned was among the last of the area woodsmen who had participated in the thirteen-foot-log drives around 1912. Speaking of those days with obvious pride, he launched into an animated recollection that captured the essence of one-time white-water work in the foothills.

I was still young, and they were driving the Middle Branch of the Grass River. I saw those guys going around in the spring and I took right after them. The fella that had the job driving it knew me. He was from South Colton.

And he says, "What are *you* doing here?"

I says, "I come over to drive river."

"*Drive river?* You know how to drive river?"

I says, "Yes." I lied to him.

Says, "Where'd you drive?"

So I told him. I'd been to Tupper Lake and knew they had logs up in there. I says, "Tupper Lake."

"Well," he says, "all right. Pick up a peavey and follow those guys."

So I started right then and *that* was done. Worked among farmers through the rest of the summer. I went in the woods in the fall. If I worked in one camp and didn't like it, I went to another. They did a lot of lumbering in this country then. I went with them to the Raquette. Woke up in the morning and was eating my breakfast on a tin plate. And this guy happened to spot me. He knew me, too. So he come over and started to talk to me.

He says to me, "What are you doing up here?"

I says, "I come up to drive."

He says, "To drive?!"

I says, "Yes. I just come off from Grass River."

Well, he commenced laughing. I had a brother that worked on the same drive, and he come over.

Ned Long, one of the last of the western Adirondack "white-water men." South Colton, N.Y., August, 1975.

So he says to this fella, "Is he up here looking for a job?"

He says, "Yes."

"Well, don't give it to him. He'll get drownded up there."

"Well, don't worry about it. I'll take care of him."

So I put the drive in. I was young. Take a chance here, take a chance there, didn't know what a chance was.

Ned worked the white water until his marriage in 1914. "That put an end to the woods," he said wistfully, "put an end to the rivers. My wife, she wouldn't stand for it—do one thing or the other." His solution was

The Linn tractor, early evidence of mechanization in the foothills lumber industry. Photograph courtesy of the Adirondack Museum.

to operate log peelers at the Raquette River Paper Company plant in Potsdam for the next two years. He spent forty-four years thereafter as a pipe fitter for the same firm. Ned Long was one among many foothills woodsmen who knew the local lumber industry at its grassroots level. And over the course of his lifetime he witnessed some sweeping changes.

Introduction of the Linn tractor into the lumber woods shortly after World War I had a profound impact upon operations. The powerful tractors utilized caterpillar treads in combination with log sled front-end steering, an innovation that greatly facilitated log hauling. Seventy-five-year-old Harold "Bub" Stowe was skilled at driving and maintaining them. Bub, who lives in South Colton, recalls that fifteen to twenty-five loads of hardwood logs was an average haul over snow-covered trails in the early 1930s. Typically, the tractors were met at loading sites where gasoline-powered cranes took over much of the log lifting formerly the burden of men alone. Trucks, in turn, transported the logs to mills sometimes many miles distant. It was the beginning of a new era.

The real change, stress Eddie and Ted and others like them, came in the late 1930s and early 1940s with the demise of the sleep-in lumber-camps that for so many years had brought men together in the woods. Recalls Ted:

Hauling four-foot pulpwood prior to the tractor and truck era. Photograph courtesy of Edward Ashlaw.

Modern-day log skidder. South Colton, N.Y., November, 1974.

Foothills lumbercamp typical of jobber operations in the 1930s. Note the gasoline pump and sawed-board construction. Photograph courtesy of Edward Ashlaw.

At the end of the thirties nobody stayed in camp anymore. Everybody stayed home and drove to it, because then they had their bulldozers, had their roads right into camp where they could drive a car right in. That made all the difference in the world. Hell, years before that, they went to camp and had to stay there or walk out. Log hauling would start right around New Year's time. Nobody'd think of going out till it was all done in the spring. And in the summer, when the bark started to be peeled—in the last part of May, or the first of June—they'd go in there and never come out till the bark peeling stopped. And then they'd probably come out for a week, and have a blowout, and go back and start cutting their pulp up and skidding it. And stay to camp.

My brother was a jobber. And the last camps he built, he said, "I just as well had not built them at all." One or two men might stay in camp. And it was no good with them staying at home. He never knew who was going to be there and who wasn't. In the morning sometimes somebody didn't come, sometimes some of them was late. Oh, hell, it weren't the same anymore when they began to bulldoze those roads and drive cars right to camp.

The days are gone when Eddie, Ted, Bub, and Ned did their part to make lumbering in the western foothills a flourishing enterprise. The whine of chain saws has replaced axe chops and the sound of two-man saws ripping through tree trunks. There is no need to lament that transition; it is a reality that elderly former loggers understand and accept. Lumbering continues in the region, but the company operations are consolidated and restricted to carefully managed timber tracts. Practices such as "integrated harvesting," now widespread, were unknown in earlier times. So were the kinds of technical skills and equipment seen employed as one drives through the backcountry. What hasn't changed much, though, is the response that these sights arouse in elderly woodsmen, some of whom, like Elroy Sochia, still cut timber on an occasional basis. Talk about the camps and associated experiences continues to stir memories and to prompt yarns.

Notes

Much has been written on American and Canadian logging. Most treatments deal with the lifestyle and lore of the workers. For an excellent overview of the Canadian heritage, see Donald MacKay, *The Lumberjacks* (Toronto: McGraw-Hill Ryerson, 1978). MacKay quotes extensively from interviews with ex-loggers, and his account reveals the close affinities of the premechanized industry in Ontario, Quebec, and Northern New York. Note also David C. Smith, *A History of Lumbering in Maine 1861–1960*, Maine Studies, No. 93 (Orono, Maine: University Press, 1972).

Several books, taken together, provide specific information on western Adirondack lumbering from the late nineteenth century to the present: Barbara Kephart Bird, *Calked Shoes: Life in Adirondack Lumber Camps* (Prospect, N.Y.: Prospect Books, 1952), Bryan, *Raquette*, pp. 101–17; Frank A. Reed, *Lumberjack Sky Pilot*, 2nd ed. (Old Forge, N.Y.: North Country Books, 1965); Albert Fowler, ed., *Cranberry Lake from Wilderness to Adirondack Park* (Syracuse: Syracuse University Press, Adirondack Museum Books, 1968), pp. 105–53; Floy S. Hyde, *Adirondack Forests, Fields, and Mines* (Lakemont, N.Y.: North Country Books, 1974), pp. 16–83; Louis J. Simmons, *"Mostly Spruce and Hemlock"* (Tupper Lake, N.Y.: Vail-Ballou Press, 1976), pp. 109–37. See also R. E. Kerr, "Lumbering in the Adirondack Foothills," *Quarterly* (St. Lawrence County Historical Association), 9 : 2 (Apr., 1964), 12–13, 15. Harold K. Hochschild, *Lumberjacks and Rivermen in the Central Adirondacks, 1850–1950* (Blue Mountain Lake, N.Y.: Adirondack Museum, 1962), and William F. Fox, *History of the Lumber Industry in the State of New York*, U.S. Department of Agriculture, Bureau of Forestry Bulletin 34 (1902; rpt., Harrison, N.Y.: Harbor Hill Books, 1976), set the foothills industry in its larger context. Periodicals like the *Northern Logger* (Old Forge, N.Y., 1963–), which had its inception in the Adirondacks as the *Lumber Camp News* (1939–52), help keep the history up to date. Back issues are available at the archives of the Adirondack Museum.

Corroborating accounts of the bedbug and lice hazards appear in Thompson, *Body, Boots & Britches*, p. 268; Fowler, *Cranberry Lake*, pp. 147–48; and MacKay, *Lumberjacks*, p. 233.

For annotation of tale types and motifs, I refer here and in the notes for the following chapter to Antti Aarne and Stith Thompson, *The Types of the Folk-Tale: A Classification and Bibliography*, 2nd rev. ed., Folklore Fellows Communications 184 (Helsinki: Suomalainen Tiedeakatemia, 1961); Stith Thompson, *Motif-Index of Folk-Literature*, rev. ed., 6 vols. (Bloomington: Indiana University Press, 1955–58), and Ernest W. Baughman, *Type and Motif-Index of the Folktales of England and North America* (The Hague: Mouton, 1966). Motifs represented in this chapter are B874.1, "Giant lice"; J1805.2, "Unusual word misunderstood"; X1291(bb), "Bedbugs drop onto man from ceiling"; X1622.3.1*, "Cold affects thermometer," for Ham Ferry's winter temperature hyperbole; and X1296, "Lies about lice," for the lice cure yarn.

3

Bunkhouse Yarns

Life in foothills lumbercamps had its light moments. As Bub Stowe put it in 1970, "There was funny things that happened in the woods, of course, same as anywhere else." We talked about some of those memorable occasions, and stories associated with them, while seated at a card table in the garage behind Bub's home. Just off South Colton's main street, the garage serves as his woodworking and machine shop. It is also a place where local men gather to reflect on days gone by. In his eighties, Bub remains one of the most respected woodsmen in his community. His modesty and unassuming manner belie his sense of humor, traits that hold him in good stead among his peers nowadays as in lumber woods of the past.

Bub recalled that morning that back in the 1930s "there was always somebody skinnin' their wind" in a foothills lumbercamp. I had heard variations of the metaphor in references to colorful talk. Bub's usage, however, was to prove especially appropriate. "I didn't stay to camp too much," he said smiling,

> but I did this one time. And this old Jim Guiney was there, and an Indian from Hogansburg. And I hadn't gone to sleep yet. They'd been working down in the shop, and they come in and was going to bed. And some fella over across the camp let the goddamnedest fart you ever heard in your life.
>
> And one fella says, "That sounded like Pete Leaf." Peter Leaf was the Indian from Hogansburg.
>
> "Oh," the other fella says, "that was a lot bigger man than Pete Leaf!" It sounded funny as hell to me. Everything else was quiet in the camp, everybody else was asleep!

Bub Stowe in a reflective moment. South Colton, N.Y., June, 1970.

And what about the storytellers? Had he heard any good yarns in the bunkhouse? He sure had. Warming up to my battery of questions, Bub continued:

Johnny was from St. Regis Falls. And he was an awful good fella and a pretty good blacksmith. And comical. He was tellin' about these two French-men over there around St. Regis Falls. They was cuttin' wood back in the woods. Pulp or something. And they went to town one Saturday night and one of them bought a dollar watch to see what time it was. And he figured the other guy could tell time.

So they got back in the woods on Monday. Got along toward noon and the fella who didn't have the watch, he says, "What time is it?"

So the guy pulls it out and he says, "There she be."

The other guy looked at it and says, "I'll be damned if she ain't." Couldn't neither one of them tell time! Johnny used to tell that and laugh.

And another: Somebody over there had a sick horse. And pretty quick the neighbor's horse come down with the same thing. So he come up and asked the guy what he give his horse when he was sick.

The guy says, "I give him a drink of gasoline."

Couple of days the guy come back. He says, "I give my horse some gasoline and he died!"

"Well," the other fella says, "so did mine!"

Bunkhouse storytellers won great admiration for their talents as informal entertainers. "There was old George Woods and old Joe Clement and them fellas," Ted Ashlaw recalls, "and they were *good* at it. They'd tell some of the goddamnedest things you ever heard." Adds Eddie, "George Woods was our neighbor. Well, he'd be back in the woods there. He'd sit and tell you stories till you went to bed at night, and not tell you the same one. He'd make them up during the day, when he was working. Every night he'd have four, five, or six that he'd tell you. You were all interested in listening, too—he'd keep you roaring right into them goddamn lies!" The best of the yarns have not been forgotten. Nor have the gifted tellers whose names remain associated with memorable narratives attributed to them.

Bunkhouse stories were more than merely entertaining anecdotes and humorous fictions. They were an index of personality, a projection of self and response to situation. Says Ted:

> Old Arthur Farmer, he talked kinda funny. And he was quite an old joker, too. And somebody was telling about going up fishing at what they call Shanley's, a little place above St. Regis Falls on the river there. Said he caught a bullhead about that long [Ted gestures to indicate about two feet].
>
> Arthur said, "You're just liable to catch anything up there." He said, "I went fishing there that night," he says, "and my line hook on something that I didn't know what it was." He said, "I pulled it up. It was a lantern. And it was lit."
>
> "Why," this guy says, "you goddamn liar!"
>
> "Well," he said, "I tell you what I do—you shorten up your fish and I'll blow out the lantern."
>
> And another: He was sitting all alone in the house, and somebody rapped on the door. And he said, "*Come in, Jesus Christ! The door ain't locked!*" The priest stepped in. "Ah," he said, "I pretty near right wasn't I, Father?"
>
> Well, you got a lot of that. There was a lot of jokes and stuff like that in camp. One and then another. Somebody'd tell a "lie" and somebody'd come and see if he could get it bigger or something.

Heralded bunkhouse storytellers usually had large repertories and a knack for spontaneous fabrication. Take George McGill, for example. Seventy-nine-year-old Frank Daniels spoke of him one afternoon in September, 1970. Frank and I spent a couple of hours together huddled around a living-room table in his Parishville home, our conversation focused on lumbercamp singers and musicians. Frank remembered some of the songs, but there was no indication that he told "lies" of the sort I had been hearing about from others. Then he casually referred to McGill, "an old man who has been dead for a good many years." Frank lowered his voice in deadpan seriousness. "He could always tell you a good story, a real good one." Frank paused. I expected only a brief after-thought. "I'll tell you one of them. It won't take me only half a minute to tell it to ya. It ain't worth repeating—it's just a story."

He said, "Years and years ago I had a friend who lived up in Idaho. And he was always writing me to come out there and go bear hunting." So he said, "I went out there."

Well, he got there. "I took along with me," he said, "a good high-powered rifle."

The friend says, "I can't go with you tomorrow. But you can take the dogs. They'll go right along with you. And the next day I can go and we can have some fun."

So George took the dogs. There was nothing to do about it. So along about ten o'clock he heard the dogs barking. And they went one way from another. And this old George said to himself, "Don't chase them too hard because you'll run yourself right to death. Wait till they come to a standstill. Then you'll know where they are."

So he waited till all the dogs weren't moving. And there was the biggest bear he'd ever seen in his life. He said, "I thought I'd seen big bears, but never saw one like that. He stood right up on his hind feet, raising his front feet. And the dogs was right in front of him there barking to beat the band." George said, "I put that high-powered rifle right on him, right in his breast there, and pulled the trigger. Not a thing happened. The bear stood right there. I fired again, and the same thing—nothing happened. The bear stayed right there and the dogs stayed right there. And finally after I fired three or four times I thought I was either going crazy or my eyes were fooling me or something. Because that bear was actually getting smaller. He shrank in size, and shrank and shrank. I didn't fire no more. All at once he got up, and he weren't much more than twice the size of a pup. Well, the dogs stayed right there barking while I rushed right up there to find out what was the matter."

There was a plant grew there called the ooglethump. And the bears loved to eat that plant. And it would get them fat. Well, in racing back and forth through the woods he had turned that bear's fat into oil. And all he'd done was punctured holes in his skin and let out that fat that had turned to liquid. And it drained out. And it took him pretty near an hour to get the dogs' feet loose from the bear's grease—it was that deep all around! [Frank gestures to indicate about six inches.]

That was one of his stories. He could tell you another in five minutes. Make them right up as he went along.

Loggers relished stories about their bosses and other people of high status to whom they were held accountable. In fact, stories about real and apocryphal activities of lumber operation foremen outnumbered all others I collected. And it wasn't only the manual labor force personnel who circulated the narratives. I was surprised at the frequency with which foremen were said to tell humorous yarns at their own expense. Strategies of image management had their place in old-time lumbering no less than in politics and corporate enterprise. Told in anecdotal form, the stories fell into two general categories: those that served to "humanize" certain bosses, and ones that elevated admirable bosses and their skills to near superhuman proportions, thus confirming the achieved status.

Of the first type, two examples suffice. I asked Ted Ashlaw one day if he had heard of Jack Bruce, whose name I had run across in a local publication. "Yes," Ted said, he remembered Bruce well. "Jack Bruce was a foreman for the St. Regis Paper Company. He was a helluva nice guy, too. An awful good fella. And he was all the time joking or saying something like that.

> One day he come down and he hired a bunch of men. We left McCarthy's and were walking up the old railroad track to Wolf Pond. I don't know how it got started, but something got started about good men.
>
> Jack said, "You know, that's something I won't admit a practice of—I never hire a man I couldn't handle."
>
> There was one big strapping young fella. Said to Bruce, "Well, I just as well be going back, because you just done that." You know, he was only fooling, but Bruce got the damnedest kick out of that.

Earlier I had gotten together with Lionel "Hep" Hepburn and several other woodsmen in Colton for an evening of reminiscence and taletelling. Hep had tactfully admonished my awkward attempts several days previous to elicit yarns. "You just can't tell them on the spur of the moment," he had said. "You've got to get into it naturally, in the course of things." Now, with the other men present, things were different.

> Old Fred Kade was a lumber boss, and he got off some good ones. He talked kind of a French dialect, but he could make himself rightly understood in English.

He got married to a local girl up here by the name of Nelly Hayes. On the first night they had to look for some hotel where they could stay all alone. Well, they got up to their hotel room and Nelly started to unpack their bag. And, of course, Fred was tuggin' and tuggin' on all these heavy things: heavy socks, heavy pants and underwear, and one thing and another. And, on the other hand, Nelly sneaks somewhere and got ready for bed in pretty good time. And she was watching Fred go through all these contortions trying to get his clothes off. It seems that she was getting a little anxious.

She said, "Oh, Fred," she says, "it doesn't seem as though we were really married."

He said, "By Chris', Nelly, you wait I get off dem sock. I make'm seem!"

All lumbercamp foremen got their share of such ribbing. It came with the job, and those who could laugh at themselves were held in high esteem, especially bosses who stood head and shoulders above their counterparts. Some did quite literally; they commanded respect and got it. According to Ham Ferry:

Big Chisholm one time, his boys went out on a weekend and come back all beat up. Chisholm, he was a great big Swede. About six foot six, a big heavy man. And the next weekend Chisholm goes down with the boys. He walks in and walks right over and picked up the spitoon and throwed it right the length of the bar. Well, by Jesus, the bartender got a little excited over that. And he says, "Why, Mr. Chisholm, what's the matter?"

He says, "You beat up my boys here last weekend."

"Oh," he says, "I kinda lost my temper."

He says, "You can hold it all right *now*, can't ya?"

Hayden "Hadie" Brown was another foreman cut from the same cloth. There is a wealth of lore about him still current among woodsmen in eastern St. Lawrence County. Indeed, in the environs of Parishville, Hadie has come to represent the lumber woods foreman as magnified folk hero.

Hadie Brown lived in Wick, in the vicinity of Joe Indian Pond near Parishville, roughly between 1905 and 1925. Sumner Lucas, lifelong resident of that locale, says that Hadie died in Saranac Lake. Like Sumner, other elderly woodsmen recall that Hadie worked for such outfits as Downey and Snell, F. A. Cutting and Son, and the Brooklyn Cooperage Company on timber tracts around Lake Ozonia and the neighboring towns of Hopkinton and Parishville. But relevant as they are, these historical details have become secondary in contemporary accounts of the man. For

Hadie Brown's reputation rests on his personal attributes and accomplishments in the woods. To hear present-day woodsmen tell of him sometimes stretches credulity, to say the least.

Otis Schofell first introduced me to Hadie Brown lore. I had heard references to the name, but little more. So I asked Otis one afternoon if he could elaborate. There was scarcely a moment's hesitation. "Hadie Brown?!" he exclaimed, eyes sparkling.

> I'll tell you a story about Hadie Brown. He was a big six-foot fella, weighed over two hundred. Stronger than a small bull moose. Instead of hauling logs on trucks through here, they used to drive them down the river. And they had a camp up beyond the new bridge in town. And a man named Ed Roach had a farm there. And they were camped there. And a big two-year-old bull there was bellowing around. Hadie went up to the bull and grabbed him by the tail. Said he could set him right on his shoulder. Grabbed him by the tail and pulled his tail out!

From then on I made a regular practice of inquiring about Hadie.

As stories about Hadie began to accumulate, I noticed how frequently they made reference to his physical size and unusual strength. Eddie Ashlaw, for example, recalled that Hadie "was foreman for Bill Downey. Good jobber, good driver. He was a strong, big man. Probably six foot four." The estimates varied with the tellings. Ned Long of South Colton remembered Hadie primarily as a boss on Raquette River log-driving operations:

> I got acquainted with Hadie. Well, finally he says, "Why don't you come and work in my boat?" I was working with this one fella, but he figured that one man was a little better than the other.
> I says to Hadie, "I can't leave that fella and go and work in your boat." Well, Hadie was a high-strung old fella. The other guy went on a vacation, and I went to work for Hadie. Well, good God. That man, I seen him up here on what they call the *sault*. I was in his boat, the bowsman. I seen him reach right down to the boat oars and snap one off just as if you'd cut them. By God, he was a powerful man. He had as much power as a horse had. Why, it was nothing for him to take one of them oars and snap the goddamn thing right off. He was a six-footer, weighed about 250 pounds.

Fay Duffy's account was analogous to tales told about other folk heroes who, like Hadie, discover their special gifts in the face of challenges.

> There was a big man. He lived up in Stark. Fella by the name of Hayden H.

Brown. He was a *big* man, about six foot seven or six foot eight, and he'd weigh around 235. But they always thought about him being the biggest coward in the world.

There was a neighbor up there by the name of Paul Brothall. And Hadie was scared to death of him. I don't know why. Hadie didn't have no nerve. And they used to do a lot of fighting—we used to see fights here in the spring of the year when the river-drivers come. With that old-fashioned alcohol in them you'd have some real battles out here.

Well, anyway, up on this Joe Indian Pond outlet they tell a story about this Hadie. He met this Paul Brothall. And Brothall told Hadie right there he was going to kill him. He said, "I am going to kill you. I've got you right where I want." He had him cornered right on the bridge at Joe Indian Pond. Of course, Hadie didn't know his strength.

Well, Hadie got his nerve up and he went right after Paul. And he almost killed him.

Hadie's father lived over there, too. His name was Harlan. And Hadie had a great byword: "Mighty Jesus, my little man, tell it while you can say it!" So Hadie went home. He says, "Father," he said, "Mighty Jesus, I just licked Paul Brothall down there. I'll go right back and lick him again if you want me to!"

Men who worked under Hadie grew to respect his strength and volatile temper. Guy DeLong told about the time "Hadie got religion":

Had a bunch of the men working for him. So Sunday morning Hadie got all cleaned up. And the boys didn't feed the calf. But they set the pail right down there. Hadie didn't see that.

So Hadie goes out. "My, my," he says, "the boys didn't feed the calf!" He went out to feed the calf, and the calf put its head in the pail and threw milk all over Hadie. Hadie says, "If it wasn't for the love of Jesus in my heart," he says, "I'd knock your goddamned head off!"

Repeatedly I heard references to Hadie's colorful epithet. "It was 'mighty' this and 'mighty' that," Ned Long emphasized as he spoke of his personal contacts with the foreman. "When you heard the first 'mighty' out of him you knew *something* was going to happen!" Frank Daniels illustrated the point:

Hadie was a great fella to tell stories. And when he got telling them he'd be awful excited. You'd have to eat dinner in the woods sometimes. And they'd bring out the dinner, and the boys would get Hadie to telling them stories to get him excited. God, he got telling and it would pass right by one o'clock.

And by and by Hadie would notice what time it was. He'd say, *"Mighty Jesus, get to the bush!"*

Hadie's ability to narrate yarns did much to endear him among the work force. His forte was the tall-tale "lie," the fantastic exaggeration that fractures reality for humorous effect. Recalled Glenn Spear, "He once told about how he had a gang of Polacks working for him in the lumber woods. 'One morning,' he said, 'it was so cold that the thermometer went four foot in the ground. I sent a gang of Polacks right down there to dig it out.' Oh, he told some awful yarns—I couldn't begin to tell you the yarns he told. He was quite a man."

Many of the "lies" now associated with Hadie celebrate his management of men and prowess as a hunter. Examples of the latter type remain especially popular among woodsmen in the foothills, for such skill continues to elicit admiration among renowned local hunters like Sumner Lucas. "He went out huntin' one day," Sumner once told me, "and he come back in. And he said, 'Mighty Jesus, I killed a buck bigger than that skiddin' horse you've got there.' Said, 'Had to crawl inside of him just to dress him out!'"

On another occasion I stopped by Bub Stowe's garage intent upon asking about Hadie. Bub and several other woodsmen were playing cards. "I've heard of Hadie Brown," he began. "A great big fellow lived in Wick. I never knew the fellow myself, but I've heard a lot about him. They tell how they put seventeen deer in front of his son one time—and Hadie only killed fifteen of them."

Later that summer Ted Ashlaw likewise got to reminiscing about Hadie:

> By Jesus, old Hadie Brown. Well, one thing I always remember was when he was tellin' about how he went huntin' up on West Mountain. "On the west side," he said, "I killed the *biggest* deer that ever run the woods. And mighty Jesus, I dressed him out and I come over on the other side." Said, "I killed one *twice* as big!" I've always thought of that a lot of times. He just killed the biggest one that ever run the woods, and then he goes and kills one on the other side twice as big.

Many foothills woodsmen recognize the obvious affinities between such narratives and the better-known canon of Paul Bunyan stories, examples of which have passed in and out of print since World War I. I found that requests for Hadie Brown material occasionally produced Bunyan yarns, and vice versa. No contact topped the outpouring of Bunyan lore I recorded one evening from Avery St. Louis, a Canton plumber. Avery told me later that he had learned the accounts both from his uncle and from reading a book. But identifying sources was of little concern to him in the immediate context of the telling. It would have been the same in the smoke-filled interior of a backwoods lumbercamp bunkhouse years earlier. Mention of the name was all the prompting Avery needed.

Paul Bunyan? In fact, I saw where Paul Bunyan died. That's what my uncle told me. Showed me the cliff by Lloyd Pond over in there. He said right over here Paul fell off a cliff seven hundred feet high. And he said Paul wore rubber soles on his boots, chained rubber heels on his boots. And he said Paul was just like a cat and landed on his feet. But when he did, he bounded back up. He said every time Paul came down he went a little higher. And they shot donuts up to him. But they just couldn't get any water to him. They said he'd been gone twenty-seven days the last time he went up and he died of thirst.

Why, yesss. Paul was out in Wisconsin when they were lumbering it off. Had a camp there and he seen that the river was drying up. Water was falling. Went down and down, a regular drought. So he went and started up the river, wondering what was wrong. Pretty soon he went up there and he found this fella sitting in the river, barefooted, and he had his feet in there damming the water up. And he had three or four pencils, and one on each ear, and he was figuring there to beat all. High speed. Paul said to him, "Who are you?"

He said, "I'm Johnny Inkslinger. Who are you?"

Said, "Paul Bunyan." Said, "What are you figuring?"

"Well," he said, "there's supposed to be thirty-six sections in that township, and there's one missing."

"Why," Paul says, "I can tell you what happened. Last year they lumbered this all off. Instead of lumbering it, I'd hook onto a section with Babe there, a section of land, and haul it down to the river and cut the timber. And haul it back." He said, "The last one, I was a little bit late. I left it overnight. And there was a flood there and washed it away."

And the time he built the sawmill. The smokestacks were so high they had to hinge them to clear the clouds.

Well, somewhere there in Texas, I forget how many miles of road was crooked. Terrible. So he hooked Babe onto one end and they turned to straighten it out. I don't know how many miles, but they put it straight anyway.

He seen a bunch of logs down in New Orleans. Floated them down the Mississippi River. When he got them down there the dealers figured they'd give him half what they agreed to. Paul said, "I won't take that." They wanted a little profit.

They said, "You can't get them back."

"Oh yes I can," he said. "Babe and I will just do it together." And they pulled them back up the river.

They tell about the states there with the lakes (you can see them on a map) that are deep in the rock. He sent Ole Olsen out there to get a set of horseshoes for Babe. And he sunk right in the rock up to his knees. And that's where those lakes are. They had to carry him back.

Oh yeah. *Awful* things. Like the time that Babe was sick there and Johnny Inkslinger told him the only thing that would cure him was whale milk. Said he'd get some up at Puget Sound there. Got a couple of whales, dammed the place up and crawled in there and milked them. Babe got better.

Said it was so hot one time the corn would pop right on the stalk. And they had to herd the cattle out there. And Jesus, they all froze to death. They thought that was snow.

Paul had a gun. He had to put salt on the bullet when he shot anything to keep the meat from spoiling until he got to it. . . .

On he went, a stocky woodsman relating incredible fictions spun out of the substance of experience half perceived, half imagined. The boundaries between the real and the fanciful, the past and the present, began to blur. I sat listening to Avery St. Louis in the soft light within a structure said to be a former lumbercamp office, my temporary residence at Sterling Pond. Avery seemed to catapult himself back into a past that remained meaningful in the present. It had become clear that the days of the foothills lumbercamps, the bunkhouses, and the men like Hadie Brown lived on in memory and talk. I knew then, as I had begun to sense earlier, that it was still possible in these surroundings to close one's eyes and hear echoes of "Mighty Jesus, get to the bush!"

Notes

Two folklore field collections by Earl C. Beck include a comparable sampling of lumberwoods yarns from elsewhere in the United States: *Lore of the Lumber Camps* (Ann Arbor: University of Michigan Press, 1948), pp. 328–42, and *They Knew Paul Bunyan* (Ann Arbor: University of Michigan Press, 1956), pp. 2–27.

Bub Stowe's yarn about Pete Leaf incorporates Motif J1250, "Clever verbal retorts: general." The watch yarn, Motif J2466.3(a), "Man who can't tell time has watch," has been collected in the Catskills by Herbert Halpert, "Aggressive Humor on the East Branch," *New York Folklore Quarterly*, 2 (1946), 92, and in the Ozarks by Vance Randolph, *Hot Springs and Hell, and Other Folk Jests and Anecdotes from the Ozarks* (Hatboro, Pa.: Folklore Associates, 1965), p. 131.

Numskull stories of this sort, including the horses and gasoline yarn (J2100, "Remedies worse than the disease"), are extremely widespread in the United States. Many may be traced to England and to various jokebooks issued on both sides of the Atlantic. Compare Thompson, *Body, Boots & Britches*, p. 158.

"Will Blow Out Lantern," Type 1920H*, and Motif X1154(c), "Man catches lighted lantern," are well traveled. For variants, see Richard M. Dorson, "Maine Master-Narrator," *Southern Folklore Quarterly*, 8 (1944), 282, and Vance Randolph, *We Always Lie to Strangers: Tall Tales from the Ozarks* (New York: Columbia University Press, 1951), p. 231. The jest involving the priest builds upon Motif J1260, "Repartee based on church or clergy."

Frank Daniels's bear story is a good example of "Münchausen Tales," Type 1889; further illustrations occur in the following chapter. Motifs include X1203, "Lie: animal's food affects him in unusual way"; X1221, "Lies about bears"; and X955(a), "Remarkable killing of bear."

The anecdotes told about Jack Bruce and Fred Kade both include Motif J1250, "Clever verbal retorts: general." French-Canadian dialect stories are extremely popular in the foothills and typically poke fun at "Canuck" twisted syntax and pronunciation. For comparative material from northern Michigan, and discussion, see Richard M. Dorson, "Dialect Stories of the Upper Peninsula: A New Form of American Folklore," *Journal of American Folklore*, 61 (1948), 113–50, and the same author's distinguished regional folklore study, *Bloodstoppers and Bearwalkers: Folk Traditions of the Upper Peninsula* (Cambridge, Mass.: Harvard University Press, 1952), pp. 99–102.

Analogues for the stories about foremen Jack Bruce, Big Chisholm, and Hadie Brown are found in Richard M. Dorson, *America in Legend: Folklore from the Colonial Period to the Present* (New York: Pantheon Books, 1973), pp. 176–84, and *Bloodstoppers and Bearwalkers*, pp. 196–204. Such local-hero yarns frequently expand upon Motifs X940, "Lie: remarkably strong man," and X972, "Lie: remarkable fighter"; Otis Schofell's accounts include X912(f), "Strength of young hero," and X953(d), "Bull's tail pulled out." For similar stories about renowned watermen, see George Carey, *A Faraway Time and Place: Lore of the Eastern Shore* (Washington and New York: Robert B. Luce, 1971), pp. 51–78. Hayden Brown's personality and deeds resulted in a good number of migratory yarns becoming associated with him. A close variant of the "Hadie Got Religion" story, for instance, has been told about Mormon preacher J. Golden Kimball; it is found in Richard M. Dorson, *Buying the Wind: Regional Folklore in the United States* (Chicago: University of Chicago Press, 1964), pp. 513–14. The hunting skill tales (Type 1889) use Motifs A526.2, "Culture hero as mighty hunter," and X1234*(a), "Large deer."

There is extensive scholarship on Paul Bunyan material and its relationship to both printed sources and oral tradition. The extent to which Bunyan stories actually achieved oral currency throughout the industry, among seasoned loggers, has been a topic of heated debate. For details on the controversy, see Daniel G. Hoffman, *Paul Bunyan, Last of the Frontier Demigods* (Philadelphia: University of Pennsylvania Press, 1952); Richard M. Dorson, *American Folklore* (Chicago: University of Chicago Press, 1959), pp. 214–26; idem, *America in Legend*, pp. 168–84; and Edith Fowke, "In Defense of Paul Bunyan," Folklore Forum Preprint Series, 3:3 (1975). Chained accounts like the one by Avery St. Louis appear in Beck, *Lore of the Lumber Camps*, pp. 338–42, and *They Knew Paul Bunyan*, pp. 4–12, 16–27. Motifs for Avery's yarns include X1237.2, "Lie: the remarkable blue oxen"; X1237.2.6*(e), "Paul Bunyan hitches Babe to end of logging road. Babe pulls it out straight"; X1237.2.8*(ab), "Babe lies down in river, damming it"; X1633.1, "Heat causes corn to pop in field. Animals think popping corn is snow, freeze to death"; X958(ga), "Lakes are imprints of feet of hero's ox"; X987(b), "Paul Bunyan drives logs upstream"; X1066*, "Lie: remarkable bookkeeper"; X1012, "Lie: person displays remarkable resourcefulness"; X1021.1(a), "Man falls with rubber boots on, bounces without stop"; X1030, "Smokestack hinged"; X1081.2*(cb), "Hauling sections to landing."

4

Big Woods, "Big Stories"

Adult woodsmen in the foothills have long found ways to fuse voca-
tion with avocation. Loggers inclined to hunting, for example, had
frequent opportunities to scout the movement of game along deep-woods
tote roads. River-drivers became authorities on prime fishing holes.
Many lumbercamp cooks welcomed the chance to vary their canned and
boiled fare with a "venison fry," a practice common enough apart from
the regulated big-game season to occasion such euphemisms for deer as
"woods beef," "mountain goat," and "long mutton."

Yet male-oriented recreation in the foothills timber has never been restricted to woodsmen with lumbering experience. In general, working-
class men who grow up in the foothills are expected to be at home in the
woods. Such familiarity is a major component of male identity. At least
that is the clear impression one gets among men from lower- and middle-
income backgrounds. And it explains, I think, why local men, much
more so than women, spend a great deal of time talking about the woods
and male recreational activities within it.

To woodsmen the environment offers something more than a forest re-
treat. To be in the woods means something special, something other than
merely a change of pace through voluntary removal from everyday domestic life in valley and foothills communities. For in woodsmen's eyes
the woods is a particularly male domain. In the woods individual men
and groups of peers confront natural phenomena, self, and other men on
male terms. Their casual talk and yarns emphasize the male pursuit of
life as defined and elaborated in outdoor contexts. A dialect story I heard
from Fred Cassel of Colton makes the point in a memorable way. Fred
called it "The Perfect Moose Caller." Friends say he "gets around with
it." His energetic rendition displayed the art of dramatic pacing and dif-

ferentiation of voices in dialogue, two hallmarks of admired North Country narrators.

There was this college professor teaching biology at Harvard. And he got interested in moose. And he thought he'd go up to Canada and find out how moose breeded and propagated, and one thing and another.

So he got up there, and he found out the way to see moose was to call 'em with a birchbark horn. But like a lot of the rest of us, he didn't have too much money. And he said, "Well, hell. If they can call them with a birchbark horn, so can I." So he made a horn and he took his canoe and paddled up and down the rivers there for about two weeks. And he called and he called and he called. But he never saw a moose.

And one day he was paddling up the shore of this lake and he saw a nice little cabin on the shore. So he pulled his canoe up in the sand and went up and knocked on the door. And a nice young Frenchwoman came to the door. Says, "Bonjour, monsieur. Bonjour."

Said, "How do you do. Have you any moose around here?"

"Yes, monsieur. Plenty moose. Beaucoup moose."

"Well," he says, "very strange." Said, "I've been paddling up and down the lakes here calling moose for two weeks and I haven't seen a moose."

"Well," she said, "you must know, monsieur, it's not every man what can call a moose. Now you take my husband, Pierre. He's the perfect moose caller. Perr-fect."

"Well," he says, "is that so. Do you suppose he'd take me with him?"

"Well of course, monsieur. Be glad for to take you."

He said, "You understand, madam, I don't want to kill a moose—I just want to see a moose."

"Yes," she said. "But you know, you go with perfect moose caller you must take *gun*."

He said, "No, I don't understand. I don't want to kill a moose."

"Yes. But if you go with perfect moose caller you must take gun."

"Well," he said, "why?"

"Well," she said, "first you go in middle of lac with canoe. And Pierre, he's make a big call, you see. That is just to wake up moose. Moose is not right there. Maybe three, four mountain away. And moose, he's hear that noise and he's come fast, *fast*. From second mountain to first mountain. And you see him there but you don't shoot. No, no, you don't touch gun. No. And then Pierre, he's give another call. He put a little more glamour on that one. But you say, 'C'est finesse.' And the moose, he's come fast, *fast*. From first mountain right up onto shore of lac. And you see him there but you don't shoot. *No, no, wait! Don't touch gun! No!* And then Pierre, he give another call. That's what you

Hunting camp near Parishville, N.Y., 1972. The club name suggests the link between real life and "big story."

call the 'Hawaiian Call.' And the moose, he's come right out on the shore of the lac. And he's pawin' the sand. And you see him there but you don't shoot. *No, no, don't touch the gun! No!* And then Pierre, he's give another call. That's what you call the 'Parisien Call.' And the moose, he swim right out in the lac. *Fifty feet* from canoe. And you see him there but you don't shoot. *No, no, wait! For God's sake, don't touch the gun now!* And then Pierre, he's give the last call. That's the 'Mon-tre-al Call.' And moose, he's climb right in canoe with Pierre! *And now you must shoot! If you don't shoot now, moose is going to seduce Pierre!*"

In a sense, the woods is an arena for foothills woodsmen, much like the "lac" in Fred Cassel's yarn. They seldom articulate that type of analogy, but it holds. The woods has an importance exaggerated beyond its mere presence as landscape. The Big Woods is a testing ground—big in its geographical expanse, the challenges it presents, and its role in shaping male experience. It is little wonder that woodsmen love to tell "big stories" ("lies," "tall tales") about events in those Big Woods. Through hyperbole, the yarns transform recognizable situations and encounters into larger-than-life confrontations, ones commensurate with the Big Woods as a heroic plane of action.

The line between the factual and the marvelous is not always clearly drawn. If one is to believe local hunters, some remarkable things happen in the woods. And it is because of these real-life events that the substance of tall tales often comes off closer to the truth than might first appear. Take, for instance, one personal-experience account as handled by Ham Ferry:

I was taking this guy out guidin' one day over to Hollywood Club. My father was caretaker there for forty years. We went out with the guy and we were walkin' down. "Jesus," I said. "Hold it, hold it. There's a buck right over there!" So he pulls and shot, and the buck flinched and away he went. I said, "Gee, I think you hit him."

"Well," he says, "I shot at him."

"But," I says, "did you see where your bullet hit? Hit about six feet this side of him on a tree." We went over there and, sure enough, the bullet ricocheted off and went right into the deer's shoulder. "Well," I says, "that's the goddarnedest thing."

"Well," he says, "I always like to play those shots off sideways."

Many of the fantastic stories identified with the Big Woods also circulate in comparable timbered regions elsewhere in the country. Yarns about insects are a prime example. They are mostly told during the late spring and summer, months when black flies and mosquitoes vie as the outdoorsman's number-one nemesis. The stories flow much like the accounts of lumbercamp lice and bedbugs, building outward from intensely serious and plausible reportage to humorous incredibility. Ham Ferry is a master of the art.

I went fishin' up on the Jordan once. We went up there and we pitched a tent. We was goin' to stay overnight. Got in the tent, and I think all the mosquitoes that was up there was in the tent. So I got out and laid right out on the knoll, out there in the woods. And it got daylight, and I started down for the brook. Well, I'll tell ya—of all the black flies and all the times I've ever been in the woods, that was the worst. It was just so thick that when you walked through you'd leave a path. And you just couldn't see. I said, "This is the end of *this* thing." We quit fishin' right there!

Well, I was down at the camp one night. Jeez, the mosquitoes was thick. And I opened the camp door and I heard this commotion out there. It was two mosquitoes out there talkin'. One mosquito said to the other, "Shall we eat him here or take him down to the swamp?"

The other one said, "Jeez, we'd better eat him here. If we take him down to the swamp all the big ones will take him away from us!"

Come fall, thoughts turn to deer hunting at gathering places like Cedar Lodge and Ham Ferry's Ham's Inn. The 1970 deer season was especially poor for local hunters. Ill luck brought frustration, and the frustration occasioned countless conversations in area taverns about deer real and imaginary. I recall in particular Friday evening, November 27, at Ham's Inn. Seven or eight middle-aged to elderly male customers moved listlessly from bar stools to tables, and back again. All were dressed in hunting clothes, their faces showing fatigue and dejection after long hours in the surrounding timber. Three women sat together in one corner; the men were preoccupied among themselves. I watched as one of the male patrons approached the bar. He seemed determined to drown his disappointment in beer. The part-time woman bartender was sympathetic.

"There hasn't been too much blood spilled this year," he said to her, taking care to emphasize the sarcastic understatement.

"No," she replied, gesturing to the counter. "But there's been a lot spilled over mahogany ridge." The exchange got a laugh from everyone. Another man picked up on the drift of the talk, adding, "I've been thinking of making track soup!" The remark brought down the house, and as the evening grew longer the elusive deer grew bigger. Had Ham been present—he was in the woods at a hunting camp, engaged, I suspect, in the same thing—it would have been only natural for him to launch into a yarn he reserves for such instances:

> There's a cut which goes up to the pond [back of the inn]. There's just room enough for a car to run up through there. And this big buck's tracks are always going up through that cut. And I had a bunch of hunters there [boarding at the inn]. And they'd go up and they'd track that goddarned buck. But I didn't tell them the reason why they never caught up with him.
>
> At last, one day somebody says, "Why can't we ever see that buck?"
>
> "Well," I says, "I'll tell ya. His horns is so big that he can't walk up through the cut. So he backs up through. And you're tracking him the wrong way all the time."

I heard it said once in Colton that "there have probably been more fish caught and deer shot over bars in the area than ever in the woods." Certainly that is true at Ham's Inn, located on Route 56 about six miles northwest of Childwold. The establishment is unimposing. Forest and a series of rivers surround it. For years it has catered to local woodsmen and, to a lesser extent, the seasonal tourist trade. The informal, home-like atmosphere of the inn helps set it apart from modern commercial facilities of the sort found increasingly in other areas of the Adirondacks. There are, as I have mentioned, other spots like Ham's Inn in the foothills. What makes "Ham's place" distinctive, like Elroy Sochia's Cedar Lodge, is its proprietor.

The more I talked with foothills woodsmen, the more I came to realize that Ham Ferry's name is virtually synonymous with references to oral storytelling. He is best known within twenty-five miles in any direction

Ham's Inn, a renowned western foothills "boardinghouse and watering hole" catering to sportsmen. Childwold, N.Y., July, 1976.

from his inn. Eddie Ashlaw summed up the reputation: "He's quite a card. Dry, witty as a sonofabitch." Few would quarrel with that tribute. Everyone who knows Ham, or about him, agrees that he is a "real character" and "a great talker who knows lots of old stories." A dozen or so visits to Ham's Inn more than convinced me that the estimation is well founded. Ham, by general consensus, is a woodsman's woodsman and a gifted artist of the spoken word. He represents in the present day the flowering of many voices from the western Adirondack woods.

Ham was about to celebrate his sixty-sixth birthday when I first met him in the summer of 1970. He is a man of medium height and husky physique, his face reflecting years of exposure to the outdoors. Animated eyes, alternately intense and inclined to twinkle, hint at his narrative skill. He was born a short distance from his place of business. After graduation from local public schools, Ham spent two years at God's Bible School in Cincinnati. He never pursued the ministry. Instead, in the early 1920s he returned to the North Country to earn money working as a logger and at manual labor on nearby construction jobs. In 1929 he began what was to be forty years of service as chief mechanic and bus driver for the neighboring school district. This employment continued until mandatory retirement in 1970. By 1953, with his wife's assistance, Ham had also assumed management of the inn. The establishment had been founded by his grandfather and previously run by Ham's father and an uncle.

Ham Ferry in familiar surroundings and pose, November, 1973.

Ham has few regrets about the life and labor he has known. One thing becomes obvious in talking with him: whatever the undertaking, the woods has always held the greatest attraction. Ham's father was an accomplished river-driver who "worked the Raquette" a short distance from the inn. In addition, his father gained local renown as a guide for hunting and fishing parties. Ham sometimes assisted. As a teenager he began to guide independently on a part-time basis. His services are still in demand, for it is said that he knows game habits as well as anyone in the region. And especially on those nights at the inn when Ham is behind the bar serving up bottled beer and whiskey shots to fellow woodsmen, stories about the locales are apt to be heard.

Such was the case on the evening of July 9, 1970, my initial effort to participate firsthand in that atmosphere. It would be one thing, I thought, to visit the inn as a "regular"—someone identified with the local scene who was accustomed to stop at the establishment. But I was a stranger, and there would be no hiding it. To add to my concern, I knew that I would be younger than most of the patrons, and, unlike them, armed with a cassette tape recorder and the specialized interests of the folklore fieldworker. Would it be possible to document anything approaching characteristic talk, tall or otherwise? I doubted it. And I was wrong.

My initiation to Ham's brand of North Country humor was rapid and unforgettable. He likes nothing better than a "little harmless fun" at the expense of unsuspecting clientele. Ham is an avid and expert bowler, and he happened to be wearing a team shirt with his name embroidered in small letters above one pocket. Stepping up to the bar, I failed to notice the identification. I explained that I was "looking for Ham Ferry, the woodsman with the stories." The bartender glanced quickly at the sole patron, who I later learned was Bill Corbett of Potsdam, and then back at me. "Certainly," the bartender said, a glint in his eyes. A little unsettled I responded, "Do you happen to be Ham?" The reply: "Certainly." Both of the men smiled broadly at my attempt at entree.

That was bad enough, but after rapidly ordering a beer I made the mistake of inquiring about a cryptic number that appeared on some matchbook spines. It read KPQ 1541. I knew that there was no local telephone exchange with that designation. Besides, the inn was unlisted in the area's phone directory. Ham had an explanation. He refused to pay the high monthly rate required to maintain service to the secluded location. The salesman who promoted the matches, however, had observed that the printing cost included a phone number in the space. So Ham's practicality and wit had prevailed. If a number was needed, the call letters for his citizen's band radio would be a viable substitute. And, of course, something to talk about.

Over the next hour and several beers, Ham, Bill, and I became caught up in an exchange that was to leave me dazzled through the duration of my field experience. What transpired shifted in a matter of several minutes from a typical barroom interview to narrative of a sort that takes place whenever, as local woodsmen put it, "Ham gets going." From my experience that usually means when Ham and other men conversant with hunting and fishing and local lore get together, social drink in hand, in the environs of the Big Woods.

Our discussion that evening began as barroom conversations often begin at that time of the year, namely about men and incidents associated with recreation in the woods. I switched on my small tape recorder and let it run continuously. Bill commented that many of the things I seemed particularly interested in came to mind "when you're out hunting or fishing." Ham agreed, and it was the right kind of moment to ask him about Hadie Brown, by then a stock question.

RDB: "Did you ever hear of a guy named Hadie Brown?"

Ham: "Oh, yeah! Sure!"

RDB: "They tell a lot of stories about him, don't they?"

Ham: "Oh, yeah, them are told . . . them are . . . sure. Christ, yeah. They tell them big stories about him."

The way Ham enunciated "big stories" left no doubt that he was familiar with the genre. By implication, the reports he had in mind were to be regarded differently than ordinary hearsay. But which of the "big stories" did he know? Asking "Do you know any of them?" brought no reply; my query failed to supply the needed associational hook on which Ham might hang one of his narratives. Bill redirected the talk to the subject of deer. Reaching for his wallet, he pulled out a well-worn photograph and turned to Ham.

Bill: "Did you ever see that one-horned deer I shot?"

Ham: "No."

Bill: "It was five points—only on one side, though. Killed him Thanksgiving time."

Ham: "He lost only one horn, or he never had any more?"

Bill: "I don't know if he had it or shed it. He only had one horn. That's all he had. On his left side [he points to the photograph]. It's a nice big five-pointer—on that side!"

In another context Bill's attenuated account might have amounted to nothing more than a sketchy outline substituting for a personal-experience narrative. But here, bolstered by observable evidence and coming on the heels of Ham's mention of "big stories," the subject matter established themes that embrace tall tales wherever told: unusual game, quirks of nature, something deviating from the norm, something different than expected or desirable. And with scarcely a moment's hesitation Ham came forth with a localized variation on a widely collected woodsman's "lie":

> They tell about . . . there's a story about Hadie Brown, about the time he ran out of buckshot. So he went out and got some cherry pits. So he went out and loaded his gun up with cherry pits. The old muzzle-loader, of course— everybody used those muzzle-loaders. Went out and he shot a goddarn deer. And he wounded him and chased him, and chased it and chased it. Couldn't get him. So next fall he come back in that popular area. And Jesus Christ, he sees the goddarnedest-looking thing he'd ever seen. He was walking along and wondering what the heck it was. At last he got around sideways and looked at it. It was the deer he'd shot at, that buck he'd shot at before. And cherry trees was growing out on both sides of him.

Ham had slipped effortlessly from experiential fact to associational fancy. Bill's photograph had provided all the stimulus needed to adapt a migratory tall tale to the purposes of local anecdote. The three of us burst into laughter. Joining in, Ham stepped aside from his role as entertainer to reveal that he, too, was after all a spectator to this implausible drama in word and image.

What about Hadie's heroic proportions and the deeds attributed to him? Was it true, I asked Ham, that Hadie was "quite a strong fellow"? Ham ran a damp cloth along the counter and reached into his repertory once again.

> Oh, yeah, he was. Big man. There's no question about that. Oh, yeah. Jesus, he was a big man. Hadie Brown. Yeah, he was a big man all right.
>
> He'd be out a-huntin', and he said, "Jesus Crimers," he said, "I went out huntin' and I killed the *biggest* buck that was in the woods. And I dressed him out and I walked around there." And he said, "I killed one just *twice* as big on the other side of the hill." So he killed the biggest one before, and he went out and killed one twice as big! They tell some of the goddarnedest stories about him.

It wasn't the first time that I heard that yarn, nor would it be the last. The fused image of man and game, each larger than life, couldn't be more appropriate. And now that the theme of fantastic hunters and hunts had been established, Ham knew how to build upon it. He paused to open a second bottle of beer, and continued:

> This Mart Moody from Tupper Lake was another one of them guys. He said, "I went out one day and here was a big flock of ducks out on Tupper Lake. And I had this good dog. And I shot. And I sent the dog out there. She was heavy with pups, and I didn't know whether I should send her out there. It was a cold day in the fall. Well, she took right off and away she went. And it got dark and she never showed up. And I got to worrying about her. I worried about that dog. She was a good dog, a real good retriever. She'd get anything I'd shot at. So the next morning I woke up and I thought I'd go see if I could find her. And I got down by the shore of the lake and I looked out. And I see something coming. And this dog, she come into shore. She had three ducks in her mouth. And behind her she had seven pups. And each one of the pups had a duck in his mouth."

Ham assumed that Bill and I would know about Mart Moody, who during his lifetime (1833–1910) was one of the most celebrated of the western Adirondack guides and storytellers. Given the content of the yarn, could there be any doubt about Moody's hunting skill, or the bond between epic-hero hunter and canine companion? Ham was well aware that his audience would take special interest in the detailing of that skill and the qualities of the prized hunting dog. So the pace of the telling was deliberate and underplayed. Bill and I were transported to Moody's side; his emotion and anxiety became ours, the situation visually tangible as a mental image.

By the time Ham concluded his Mart Moody story something else had happened as well. What began as a mixture of anecdote and "big story" about Moody had changed, or so it seemed, to a personal-experience narrative by him through the voice and person of Ham Ferry. The narrative point of view had steadily yet subtly shifted from third to first person. Ham in effect had become the center of attention through the medium of his stories about woodsmen counterparts. He had coerced us willingly into watching experience become manipulated and distorted from his vantage point.

Bill, more than I, was atuned to what had taken place. He had seen it happen before in Ham's company, and he immediately seized upon the opportunity.

Bill: "I thought you were going to say 'Canadian geese' [in the duck hunting story]. They're a lot easier to pick, though, aren't they?"

Ham: "Ah, Jesus! Don't ever talk about geese. Jesus Christ Almighty. I never in my life—oh, that guy almost shot me!"

Ham and Bill burst into knowing laughter. "This guy I know loves to hunt," Ham said in a clarifying aside to me. "He don't like to hunt deer, but he loves to hunt ducks!" Then he continued.

> So I said, "Jesus, I know where there's a bunch of geese."
> He says, "You do?"
> I says, "Yeah."
> He says, "You'll take me up there?"
> I says, "Sure." I says, "You got a duck stamp?"
> He says, "No."
> I says, "I won't take ya unless you got a stamp. I don't want to get tangled up with the law or nothin'." So he went down to the post office to get a duck stamp, down to Potsdam, see. Had to go to Potsdam. He had to go clear down to Potsdam to get a duck stamp [i.e., a drive of about thirty miles northward from the inn, much of it over winding and tedious roadbed]. Well, anyway, he went down and got a duck stamp.

We were driving basketball players and had to wait for about two hours for their practicing. So we jumped in his car and we goes up there to where I knew the geese were, to where the geese was on the pond. So, Jesus, I walk all around through the marsh and got around to where they were swimmin' along.

And he said to me, he said, "*Jesus Christ!*" He was as excited as a guy with a deer. Christ, *I* wasn't more excited. He was just shaking like this [Ham gestures in exaggerated fashion]. "Shall I shoot? Shall I shoot?"

"Well," I said, "Jesus, if I wanted to kill any I think I'd start shootin' pretty soon." So he pulls: *bang! bang! bang!* And two of 'em fell. I mean, they stayed right there. Well, we had to go back and get a boat to get out in the pond to get 'em. So I went back and got my brother-in-law's boat, and went out and got the geese, and brought 'em in, and got 'em in the boat and started for shore.

And he says, "Here, you take one."

I says, "All right, I'll carry one." And as I was walkin' along (we were going to the car) I thought to myself, Jesus, both of them geese was shot in the head, both of them. There wasn't a goddarned piece of shot anywhere in 'em—only in the head. So I kept peelin': one, two, three, four, five, six, seven layers of feathers and I hadn't got to the hide yet. I said to myself, I says, I don't want no part of *this!* So we put them in the car and go back down. Picked up the kids and brought them home.

And we got down there and he says, "You can take one of 'em."

I says, "Nah, I don't care much for geese or anything. You take them and just cook one and give me a taste, that's all." (I never had any geese either.) So I said, "I don't believe I care much for 'em."

That was on a Friday night. Saturday he started pickin' the geese. He had a whole barrel of feathers and he hadn't had one picked yet! Kept pickin' and a-pickin'. Jesus Christ!

Monday mornin' he comes in. He said to me, he says, "You sonofabitch."

I said, "What's the matter with you?"

He says, "You knew about them geese."

I said, "Jesus, I didn't know nothin'. I've never been anywhere near 'em before."

"Oh," he says, "there must be somethin'. You would have taken the goose if you hadn't have known."

He had the awfullest time gettin' them feathers off. He couldn't get 'em off. Why, he dipped them in hot water. Why, they was so goddarned thick it didn't even penetrate at all. Never penetrated them. At last he got the feathers off—I guess he skinned 'em to end it off. All you got to do is say somethin' like "How about going goose hunting?" He'll say, *"You go to hell!"* I'm telling you, I

never seen so many feathers in all my born days, ever. And none of them pellets went into that thing—only the ones that hit 'em in the head. And you could see the pellets hitting them all over out there on the pond. They [the geese] wasn't in the air; they were sittin' on the pond. He shot three times and they were all hit right in the head, the two he got. And the other ones got up and flew. They were just bouncin' right off, them pellets, bouncin' right off the feathers.

Ham Ferry, guide and raconteur, was at center stage. He had completed his personal-experience narrative, had clothed it as a person-centered anecdote, and had related it in a way that verged on tall tale. Indeed, was it all a "lie"? There was no way of determining at that moment how true the story was (I later learned from a trustworthy correspondent that the incident had, in fact, occurred). It was, after all, a great entertaining story precisely because of the artful telling. There was Ham, the knowledgeable and law-abiding guide, the archetype of his breed: a woodsman who knew how to maintain the kind of hunting composure gained only through years of firsthand experience, who knew when and how to put one over on the best of friends, yet at no one's real expense. And there was Ham's hunting companion: a sportsman who went out of his way to get himself into the very predicament that Ham, in his wisdom, went out of his way to avoid, who came off the novice where Ham came off the cool professional, who remained incredulous at his own folly to the end but suspected full well that he had been the victim of some fun on Ham's terms. It was a guide's tale par excellence.

Certainly the spinning of the account enhanced Ham's personal prestige. He may have consciously intended that. Yet the story's immediate message, one that Ham knew Bill and I could appreciate, was that Big Woods events sometimes do take on implausible and fabulous qualities. The "big story" genre merely capitalized on inherent potential.

Ham opened yet another round of beers. He did it with a flair, for by now that small act had become a stylized part of the storyteller's performance and integral to it. Moving to the center of the bar, Ham resumed with a second Mart Moody yarn of the migratory variety:

"This Moody, Mart Moody, he's from Tupper Lake. That guy was one of them old-time characters. Take and bend his gun around and walk around a hill and keep shootin' right around there. The deer would be layin' there just piled right up on top of each other. Like cordwood."

Bill couldn't resist interjecting one of his own favorites. But he faced a tough competitor, and he had no sooner begun than he found himself "matching lies" in a brief impromptu contest.

Bill: "Wonder if he [Moody] ever caught a bear? You know how to catch a bear, don't ya?"

Ham: "Yeah: catch your finger in him."

Bill: "Yeah, well, there's another way, too. Christ, in the wintertime you go out and go out on a lake. Cut a big hole in the ice. And you get around there and ya take green peas. And ya stick them all the way around the hole."

Ham: "Yeah?"

Bill: "And leave 'em there, you see. When the bear comes along he gets down there and he starts eatin' the peas, you know."

Ham: "Yeah?"

Bill: "And you walk up behind him and kick him right in the ice hole! And that's the way you catch a bear."

Ham: ". . . 'Yeah,' he says, 'Jesus, I run an awful ways. Three miles. I run for three miles with my finger in the bear's ass, and I couldn't get close enough to put the crook in it!'"

Ham was not to be outdone. As the hour wore on, and the talk changed from memorable hunting to memorable fishing, Ham drew on what seemed an inexhaustible stock of stories. It had become evident that virtually any associational cue keyed to the general theme would pay off in entertainment. To introduce them, as Bill had done, was a convention in the routine. There was no reason to refrain from an elicitation technique that I had initially regarded as necessary but wholly artificial. So I asked Ham if he knew "any of those 'big stories' about fishing, where you throw a line in the water and get more than you bargained for?" The question paid off far beyond what I anticipated.

One time a guy and I went up to Sevey's [formerly a boardinghouse similar to Ham's Inn, several miles to the south]. A guy come in here who I used to work with on the road. We went up to Sevey's. There was two fishermen in there that had just come in to Sevey's. We knew they were fishermen—they were all dressed up. They had all these flies hangin' all over them and, Christ Almighty, big hip boots and all! So we started in.

He [i.e., Ham's companion] says, "Jesus Crimers, it's too bad I didn't bring Big Bertha up here with me today."

I says, "Why? What's the matter? Why didn't you bring her?"

"Well," he says, "the game warden has got to where he won't let me carry her around because he knows I'm going to take her out and go fishin' with her."

"Well," I says to him, "what's the matter with that?"

"Well," he says, "they found out all I had to do was turn the worm loose out

in the river, and I'd stand along and thump the fish over the head. She'd chase them right into shore."

These guys were sittin' right there, takin' it all in. Goddarnedest story! We all made 'em up as we went along, you know. He'd get one, and then I'd come along and tell one.

So a guy from Rochester come up here one time. And he was going to go fishin'. He brought some night crawlers. And honest to Jesus, I've seen big night crawlers, but I'd never seen nothin' like 'em. Those goddarned night crawlers were a foot long. They were as big as your thumb. I'd never seen such night crawlers. So I took them out and dumped them in the garden.

So somebody come along one day and said to me, said, "You got any worms?"

I said, "Yeah, I got some night crawlers out there." I says, "They're offspring from Big Bertha." I says, "She just had a few extras the other day." So I went out there and right there I dug them up. There they were, all in one place! I said, "Big Bertha always comes out and lets me know when she puts off a bunch of offsprings."

So somebody come in here one day and bought some of them corn sticks [Ham points to some packaged food sold over the bar.] He said to me, he said, "Jesus, where do you get them?"

"Why," I says, "from Big Bertha's offsprings. I take them and chop them up and dip them in cracker crumbs, and dip them in the goddarned hot grease. And there you are."

He says, "I don't believe I want any more."

I've had more fun over Big Bertha. Tall stories. Jesus Christ!

Bill and I looked at each other, then at Ham, then back at one another. Neither of us could have predicted that kind of exposure to Ham's creative process, to "big stories" in the making. The recipe had been made explicit: take ingredients of topical interest and familiar Big Woods experience, add elements of the fantastic, and blend in the presence of receptive auditors. Ham was more than a bartender and entertaining minstrel of a foothills inn; he was a gourmet cook in the fine art of the spoken word.

The hour drew to a close not long thereafter. Bill paid his bar tab and departed. I lingered on late into the evening, watching Ham interact with a series of new patrons and enraptured as he fielded my questions during the lulls. But I had already heard enough to know that Ham would figure prominently in my compilation of voices, be they past or present, from the Adirondack woods.

Notes

Fred Cassel's "The Perfect Moose Caller" hinges on Motif H1214, "Quest assigned because of hero's knowledge of animal languages." Ham Ferry's story about the ricocheted bullet incorporates X1122.4*, "Lie: ingenious marksman shoots bank shot." The several insect yarns, including Type 1960M, "The Great Insect," use Motifs X1286.1, "Lie: the large mosquito"; X1286.1.5(a), "Mosquitoes confer about eating man"; and X1286.4*, "Thick mosquitoes."

For a concise history and analysis of the tall tale genre, see Gerald Thomas, *The Tall Tale and Philippe d'Alcripe*, Memorial University of Newfoundland Folklore and Language Publication Series, Monograph Series, No. 1, and Publications of the American Folklore Society, Bibliographical and Special Series, Vol. 29 (St. John's: Memorial University of Newfoundland, 1977), pp. 1–48. For portrayals of other woodsmen and the "lies" they tell, see Thompson, *Body, Boots & Britches*, pp. 128–42, 289–93; Herbert Halpert, "John Darling, a New York Münchausen," *Journal of American Folklore*, 57 (1944), 94–106; C. Richard K. Lunt, "Jones Tracy: Tall-tale Hero from Mount Desert Island," *Northeast Folklore*, 10 (1968), 5–62; and Kay L. Cothran, "Talking Trash in the Okefenokee Swamp Rim, Georgia," *Journal of American Folklore*, 87 (1974), 340–56.

An excellent discussion of tall-tale narrative style, based on material collected from a bait store owner comparable to Ham, is found in Patrick B. Mullen, *I Heard the Old Fishermen Say: Folklore of the Texas Gulf Coast* (Austin: University of Texas Press, 1978), pp. 130–48. Like Mullen, my understanding of the storytelling techniques benefited from a reading of Richard S. Tallman, "'You Can Almost Picture It': The Aesthetic of a Nova Scotia Storyteller," *Folklore Forum*, 3 (1974), 121–30. Tallman shows how the narrative artistry of Robert Coffil, from Blomidon, Nova Scotia, is tied to correspondences between life as lived and perceived, and narrative development that allows "the listener and teller to picture in detail the story as it progresses from one scene to another" (p. 127). He concludes that an effective narrative engages performer and audience mutually in a "visual drama in the mind's eye. The more vivid and detailed the mind-picture is, the better the story" (p. 128).

Ham's lead-off story for the evening I report is Tale Type 1889C, "Fruit Tree Grows from Head of Deer," a Münchausen standard among woodsmen in many areas of the United States. The core motif is X1130.2, "Fruit tree grows from head of deer shot with fruit pits." Type 1889H, "The Obedient Dog," combines X1215.9, "Lie: obedient or dutiful dog," with X1212, "Lie: animals inherit acquired characteristics."

For details about Mart Moody's life and examples of tall tales attributed to him, see Thompson, *Body, Boots & Britches*, pp. 289–92, and Maitland C. DeSormo, *The Heydays of the Adirondacks* (Saranac Lake, N.Y.: Adirondack Yesteryears, 1974), pp. 245–58.

In his yarn about the geese, Ham elaborates upon Motif X1258.2, "Tough goose. Goose with impenetrable skin." Later, in Type 1890E, "Gun Barrel Bent," he localizes X1122.3.1*, "Lie: hunter bends gun barrel in curve, shoots around mountain, kills game out of sight." The exchange of bear stories plays upon

X1124, "Lie: hunter catches game by ingenious or unorthodox method"; Ham tops the contest with a bawdy variant, coupled with X1796.2*, "Lie: running ability." For the "Big Bertha" material, see Motifs X582*, "Jokes about tourists"; X1156, "Lie: unusual method of catching fish"; and X1346.1*, "Lies about earthworms."

Ham is also well known for his oral recitations of folk monologues and popular verse; Canadian poet Robert W. Service (1874–1958) ranks as a favorite author. I discuss this aspect of Ham Ferry's artistry in "Verse Recitation as Barroom Theater," *Southern Folklore Quarterly*, 40:1–2 (Mar.–June, 1976), 141–68, in a special issue, "Monologues and Folk Recitation," that Kenneth S. Goldstein and I co-edited.

5

Lumbering and Foothills
Folksong Tradition

Traditional folksongs and folksinging have been much less durable than yarns and oral storytelling in the North Country. That pattern is not unique, of course, to northern New York State. Changes in popular taste, stimulated largely by mass-media entertainment and especially the commercial recording industry, have altered the currency of grassroots Anglo-American folk music across the United States. Elderly Adirondack woodsmen recognize the transition; they have lived through it. Yet many of them also look back to the days when lumbermen "woods singers" captivated local audiences in lumbercamp bunkhouses and selected barrooms and homes.

There is no denying that things have changed in the western foothills since World War II. The isolated sleep-in lumbercamps are gone. Many woodsmen still frequent area barrooms, but the faces of men who know the "old songs" are much less commonplace. The atmosphere at most of these spots is different, too. Packaged entertainment is nowadays standard fare along with the customary whiskey shots, schnapps, brandy, and beer. Television sets and coin-operated table shuffleboard games are ubiquitous. For a quarter one can hear the latest 45 rpm Nashville release on a sophisticated jukebox. It wasn't always that way. Once there was time and desire for live, unaccompanied renditions of folk ballads like "The Jam on Gerry's Rock" and "The Cruel Ship's Carpenter." And there were men who knew how to sing them for appreciative listeners.

It's not surprising to find a heritage of singing among foothills lumbermen. Loggers across the United States and Canada produced a huge corpus of songs dealing with their experience. But lumbermen, like cowboys, sailors, miners, and railroad workers, were also inclined to sing

Wilfred Monica, a logger who "had a song for every purpose." Norwood, N.Y., August, 1974.

about more than their immediate occupation. In the western Adiron-dacks, as elsewhere, the songs and their sources included imported British and Irish folk ballads and lyrics; native American ballads and songs, among them localized topical compositions of ephemeral currency; comic ditties; bawdy or obscene descriptive pieces; songs from the nine-teenth-century stage and music hall; turn-of-the-century Tin Pan Alley tearjerkers; popular sentimental and patriotic songs of World War I vin-tage; and various items learned or derived from song sheets, pocket song-sters, newspapers, early commercial phonograph records, and radio.

To learn about that heritage as known from firsthand exposure, one turns to woodsmen like Frank Daniels of Parishville. I met Frank early in my fieldwork. Following leads to former loggers like him had begun to be productive. Clearly there were men who remembered the "old songs," although it took some looking and luck to find them. Always there was the anticipation of discovering contacts who admitted to being "singers" and who were willing to perform.

Frank, as it turned out, confessed to being more of a listener than an entertainer. He had worked in the local lumber woods between 1904 and 1913, later serving for forty years as town superintendent of highways. Wiry and suspendered, he looked the part of a man who had spent a good many days in the outdoors. "The singing mostly was done in the lumbercamps to make amusement for the fellas at work," he recalled. "Maybe some fellas would play on the mouth organ, some would sing, some would dance. Once in a while a fella would bring in a violin. One time a new fella came who had a set of bagpipes, and he entertained. They didn't have much amusement—there was no radio in those days." Other men were to single out imitative instrumental music (e.g., placing a forefinger inside one cheek, distending the jaw, and using the free hand to tap out a jig rhythm on the cheek's exterior), harmonicas ("mouth organs"), and the Jew's harp ("jaws harp"). Frank talked about what he could verify from his own experience.

It became obvious that Saturday afternoon that songs associated with lumbering meant something special to Frank and his wife, Tess. I mentioned some titles, anxious to get a sense of the local repertory. The query brought immediate response. "My wife's father knew most of them songs," Frank remarked, "and he'd sing 'em to home." He left his living room briefly and returned with a thick daybook in hand. Years earlier the couple had begun to save newspaper printings of familiar verse. Some of the material had appeared in the "Old Favourites" column of the *Family Herald*, a rural-oriented Canadian weekly published in Montreal. I opened the volume to several well-fingered pages. The clippings were glued in columns, in effect a homemade compendium of ballads, songs, and popular poetry. Items included "Sam Bass," "The Sailor's Alphabet," "You'll Never Know a Mother's Love Again," "Whispering Bill" by Irving Bacheller, "Noble Lads of Canada," "Nobody Cares for the Poor," "Life's Railway to Heaven," "The Drummer Boy's Burial," "May the Grass Grow Green above You," "The Little Brown Cot," "Stick to Your Mother, Tom," "May I Sleep in Your Barn Tonight, Mister?," "Only an Old Song," by Benjamin S. Parker, "The Basket Maker's Child," "The Old Front Door," "The Jam at Gerry's Rock," "Ain't I Crazy," "Oh Dem Golden Slippers," "The Mariner's Dream," "The *Flying Cloud*," "Where the Silvery Colorado Wends Its Way," "In the Baggage Coach Ahead," "The Patchwork Quilt," "When the Work's All Done This Fall," "Cold Harbor 1864," "Twenty-one Years," "The Letter Edged in Black," "Floyd Collins," and "Bad Companions."

Frank and Tess peered over my shoulder and smiled, caught up in fond memories. "Those are lumbercamp songs," Tess began. "My father worked for a lumbercamp, and he learned a number of songs in the camps. When he was out doing his chores you could hear him singing his songs. He'd sing most generally when he got out milkin'—get alone by himself." In short, her father was one of the links in the local mesh of woods and domestic song tradition.

Such men had a profound impact as entertainers. Often their performances in domestic settings provided the inspiration and model for other singers. Ted Ashlaw, to whom I shall return later, spoke of one formative occasion:

> There was an old fella that lived next to my father up on the Lake Ozonia Road. Old man Monica. And oh, he was a good singer! But it was all in French, and at that time I'd growed up and I didn't understand half of it. But I could set and listen to that man sing all day and all night. Boy oh boy, what a voice! And couldn't he sing!
>
> And I'll never forget one night he was over to my folks' and my father asked him to sing some old song they used to sing together or something. And he couldn't think of it, couldn't get it together. Anyway, that night after they'd drank what they wanted and they went to bed, that old man sung that song after he went to sleep. And he sung every bit of it, right in his sleep. Must have been thinking of it when he laid down. I don't know what his song would have sounded like in English, but it certainly was something!

George Guthrie of Canton was another lumberman who sang at home as well as in the woods. I learned about him from his son, Claude, a retired baker locally admired for his fiddling. Claude reminisced over coffee at his kitchen table one evening in the spring of 1971. "I never gave it much thought when I was a kid to home and grew up," he reflected.

> Dad would sing for entertainment. We never had a radio or anything in those days. He'd get out on the porch and sing. Smoke his pipe, you know—take a few puffs on it and sing another verse or two. My dad knew several of those old, old pieces: "After the Ball," "Casey Was Dancing with a Strawberry Blond," "The Baggage Coach Ahead," and hundreds of those. He was a beautiful singer. He was a smoker but he never hacked or hemmed at all. And he'd sing all night and never sing the same song twice.

From the description I suspected that George Guthrie got around with his songs. I asked about contexts other than the household. "He would go to a congregating place," Claude replied, "a hotel, barroom or anything, and they'd tease him to sing." The material fell into several categories, what Claude termed "lumberjack songs" (e.g., "The Bonneshai River"), "tragedy songs" (e.g., "The Lake of Shilin"), "liquorish songs" (e.g., "The Drunkard's Doom"), and "comedy songs" (e.g., "An Old Gray Ghost Hitched at a Post"). Claude recited text fragments as he enumerated, now and then launching into a tune as he reached into the past. He consented to sing one of his father's favorites. It happened to be a chestnut from the lumbering canon, one "for the lumberjacks." The piece very likely accrued its logging content in Maine, in the early to mid-1800s, among sailors who worked in the woods during the inclement winter months. The song's progenitor is known as "The Sailor's Alphabet."

THE LUMBERJACK'S ALPHABET

A is for axes, I suppose you all know;
B is for boys that choose them so;
C is for chopping we first did begin;
D is for danger we ofttimes were in.

So merry, so merry, so merry were we,
No mortals on earth were as happy as we;
Hi derry, ho derry, hi derry down,
Give a shantyboy whiskey and nothing goes wrong.

E is for the echoes that through the woods rang;
F is for foreman, the head of our gang;
G is for the grindstone, so swiftly turned round,
And *H* is for the handles, so smoothly worn down.

I is for the iron that stamped our pine;
J is for the jobbers that all fell for wine;
K is for keen edges our axes did keep;
L is for the ladies kept everything neat.

M is for moss that chinked our camps;
N is for needles that mended our pants;
O is for the owls that hooted all night,
And *P* is for the pine that always fell right.

Q is for the quarreling we'd never allow;
R is for the river our timber did plow;
S is for the sleds so stout and so strong,
And *T* is for the teams that hauled them along.

U is for usage we put ourselves to;
V is for the valleys we cut our roads through;
W is the woods that we left in the spring,
And now I have sung all I'm going to sing.

So merry, so merry, so merry were we,
No mortals on earth were as happy as we;
Hi derry, ho derry, hi derry down,
Give a shantyboy whiskey and nothing goes wrong.

Woodsmen like George Guthrie and his son often had multiple talents as music makers. I found no evidence in the foothills that men were hired on lumber crews solely in the capacity of entertainer. However, such ability sometimes proved advantageous when looking for work. Take the case of Claude's father. "I talked with old Jimmy Spears one time," Claude recalled, settling back in his chair.

Mr. Spears said that at one time he had this spring river-drive on. And he went up and he says to the foreman, "All the help showed up?"

"Yeah," he says, "I guess so." He says, "George Guthrie come?"

"No."

"Well," he says, "as soon as he comes give him a job."

"Well," he says, "we've got enough men."

"Give him a job anyway. He's worth his wages keeping the punks feeling good. He plays the mouth organ, he sings, and he dances. And he's a good river-driver."

About that time my old man came along with a pair of shoes over his back. This foreman says, "We'll have a little fun with him."

So he come up and says, "You got your help all picked?"

"Yup, got all the help I need. Matter of fact, I got a little too much!"

"Hell. Well, I guess by Jesus you'll have to go, 'cause I've come up here to work on the river-drive and I'm going to stay!"

Reports vary in the foothills on the number of men who actually sang in bunkhouses. Ted Ashlaw, for example, claims that "there wasn't too many that would sing in camp." His brother Eddie, on the other hand, represents the opposite extreme in his insistence that "Jesus Christ, if you knew a song or anything, at night why you sat on the bunk and sang. It's all the entertainment you had, and maybe a harmonica if somebody might have one." I am inclined to believe both brothers. In view of what they and other contacts claimed, the number of men who regularly performed appears to have been much smaller than often suggested in romanticized accounts of logging. Men at rest in bunkhouses were not a singing and dancing throng, although on occasion they did sing and dance. And the demands of the rigorous work schedule, plus sheer exhaustion, tended to limit that lumbercamp singing to the customary respite on Saturday and Sunday nights.

The consensus, then, is that most crews were likely to include at least one man, and sometimes several, who met the criteria of what Eddie defined as a "singer." In his words, "any of them that *could* sing in camp, sang. If you found two or three in a camp of thirty to forty men, that's about all you'd get. What'd I look for? Well, if one had a voice, and cared to sing at all, and knew any songs." Often, such singers expected a little playful banter as inducement to perform; a little coaxing, and anticipation, were good for an artist's ego.

While songs were carried back and forth from household to woods, the latter male environment lent itself to material considered inappropriate in mixed company. To slight the "dirty songs" is to misrepresent the singing tradition. Ted and I got to talking about the items one day. He mentioned a piece entitled "Cousin Nellie," but declined to sing it because some women and neighborhood children were in an adjoining room. "I'll always remember that song" he said, breaking into a laugh. "I was in camp, and there was a preacher that come up into camp. And those sonofabitches, you know, they had me singing or something all the time in there anyway. And they kept at me to sing a song. And I started that one. 'Course, on the start it sounds all right. I'll never forget. That preacher kept crowding up to get closer. There was these long benches along the bunks. And he got pretty well up close to me. And I got to the other end of the song, and then he got up and got the hell out!" Later, when Ted sang the song for me in private, I could envision the uproar it must have created.

COUSIN NELLIE

I watched my cous-in Nel-lie for man-y, man-y day, I watched her bod-y at-ten-tive, like-wise her win-ning way. Her charm-ing eyes of pas-sion, most gen-tle as a dove, And I oft-times thought it would be nice to teach her how to love. Var. 5-6

I watched my cousin Nellie for many, many day,
I watched her body attentive, likewise her winning way.
Her charming eyes of passion, most gentle as a dove,
And I ofttimes thought it would be nice to teach her how to love.

"Oh, love is but a passion," most tenderly I said,
"And if I teach you now, you'd turn your pretty head.
You would not give your passion, nor give yourself to me."
"Oh Harry," cousin Nellie said, "pray try me once and see."

I took that silken wrapper from off her snowy breast,
And many and many a kiss on those bounty lips I pressed.
With one hand slowly ascending, I reached between her thighs,
And felt that soft and hairy spot where true-love passion lies.

I then pulled peter out gently and I laid him in her hand,
I bid her to direct him, but she needed no command.
And then to deteeve her I reached home with a shove;
"Oh Harry," cousin Nellie said, "what pleasure it is to love!"

There scarcely a day goes by me now but what she'll come to me,
And with her clinging to me, she'll walk to the leaning tree.
She'll spread herself before me there and spread that venus bare;
"Oh Harry," cousin Nellie said, "true love lies only there."

Playful license in lumbercamps was at best a fleeting substitute for life beyond the woods. Particularly during the premechanization years, payday reintroduced loggers to "civilization." Some men returned to their families and homes in surrounding communities. Others, especially itinerants and bachelors, had one thought in mind: to raise hell during the break in the seasonal work cycle. Guy DeLong of Parishville recalled the stir created by the annual log-drivers on the West Branch of the St. Regis River. "It was quite a town here when the drives came through. Another drive went down to Stockholm. I'd go down there when the old hotel was runnin'. The log-drivers and all would fight and kick each other with caulked shoes—knock the little town in for about a week there."

The "blowouts" occasioned mixed feelings among participants. As Ted puts it,

I've seen guys go in camp, get a stake, and come out and say, "I've got to get some clothes." Come out and get in Tupper Lake and go and buy themselves maybe forty or fifty dollars worth of clothes. Go right over to the hotel and drink up everything they had, and then sell that forty or fifty dollars worth of clothes for another bottle. Come back to camp with the same clothes they went out with. Oh, I've seen that time and again. You might better drink it all in the first place—you'd have more to drink! I never could see that, sellin' my clothes for somethin'. But there's a lot of 'em did.

In effect, hotel barrooms and taverns catering to the labor force amounted to a community extension of the bunkhouse. But there was an important difference. Most lumbercamp bosses enforced strict prohibitions against alcohol consumption. As Frank Daniels observed, "Sometimes there'd be a handwritten sign in the camp saying, 'Anybody found with liquor in their possession will be turned out and paid a dollar a day.'" No woods boss could afford alcohol-induced dissension in his work force. That is not to say that men didn't drink covertly. Smuggled bottles and illicit moonshine made their way into many camps. Yet it was a touchy affair, one alleviated when foothills loggers drifted into public spots like Sevey's Hotel and Ham's Inn, the Evergreen Hotel at Cranberry Lake, and the Grand Union Hotel at Tupper Lake Junction. The places were as numerous and scattered as the local operations, and they were a focal point for informal entertainment.

Take, for example, Sevey's Hotel in the southeastern corner of St. Lawrence County. Ted described what it was like thirty to forty years ago, the period when truck transportation of logs had begun to bring woodsmen together in barrooms with greater frequency. "You used to get in there and there was some singing and banjos. That used to be a great stopping place for us pulp haulers. We'd get in one of them barrooms, and Eddie would have me singing there sometimes for six or eight hours, when he was lumbering and I was working for him. Some guys would be all for one, another guy would be all for someone else. Like that 'Foreman Young Monroe.' I probably sung that thing maybe five thousand times! 'Course, it was a lumberjack song."

Like his friend Wilfred Monica of Norwood, woods singer Ted Ashlaw "had a song for every purpose." No text enjoyed greater sustained popularity than "The Jam on Gerry's Rock," to which Ted refers. Most of my field contacts were familiar with the piece. But Ted's rendition, recorded in 1970, was especially memorable, a majestic and bard-like performance. He straightened in his kitchen chair, draping one arm over its back. Then, tilting his head slightly forward in a pose adopted many times thereafter, Ted began:

THE JAM ON GERRY'S ROCK

Come all you true-born shantyboys, wherever you may be,
I would have you pay attention and listen unto me,
Concerning one young shantyboy who was manful, true, and brave,
While breaking jams on Gerry's Rock, where he met his watery grave.

It was early on a Sunday morning, as you will soon now hear,
Our logs were piled up mountain high, we could not keep them clear.
Our foreman cried, "Turn out, brave boys, with your hearts all void of fear,
We'll break the jam on Gerry's Rock and for Agonstown we'll steer."

Now, some of them were willing, while others they hung back;
To work upon a Sunday, they didn't think it right.
While six of our brave Canadian boys did volunteer to go,
To break the jam on Gerry's Rock with their foreman, young Monroe.

They had not rolled off many a log when Monroe to them did say,
"I would have you be on guard, brave boys, for those logs will soon give
    way."
He had no sooner spoke those words when the logs did break and go,
And carried off six of our brave men and the foreman, young Monroe.

It was early on a Monday morning, to our sad grief and woe,
To search for our dead comrades to the river we did go.
We found one headless body, to our sad grief and woe,
All crushed and mangled on the beach was the head of young Monroe.

We picked it from its watery grave, smoothed back his coal-black hair;
There was one fair form amongst them whose cries would rend the air,
There was one fair form amongst them, a girl from Saginaw town,
Whose mourns and cries would rend the skies for her true-love that was
    drowned.

Miss Clara Benson was her name and she dearly loved her friend;
She lived with her widowed mother, down by the river bend.

All of her lover's wages the boss to her did pay,
Besides a large subscription from the shantyboys next day.

Miss Clara did not survive long to her sad grief and woe,
For scarce six months was over when death called her to go.
Ere scarce six months was over when her body did lay low,
And her last request was granted, to be laid by young Monroe.

Now, come all you true-born shantyboys who wish to go and see,
To a little mound by the river bend there stands a hemlock tree.
The shantyboys cut the woods all round where two lovers do lie low:
Miss Clara Benson is the maid, and her lover *young Monroe.*

The special appeal of such songs is understandable. More than a tribute to occupational heroism and sacrifice, they were a constant reminder
of the dangers on foothills rivers. The association was immediate and
lasting, a kind of loggers' *memento mori.* As Ham Ferry once put it, the
ballads told a story "which could have happened to me, could have happened to you, could have happened to anybody." He added, "That's the
type that kinda gets under my skin more than the rest of 'em." Most lumbermen woods singers shared his view. Ted, for example, often speaks of
his personal identification with "The Jam on Gerry's Rock": "There was
two guys I knew well—Jack and Sam Arnold. Well, them two brothers
drownded on the Beaver River on a river-drive. One of 'em drownded
one year and one of 'em drownded the next. I imagine it was probably
the pulp that put them down, and they couldn't get back out. Hell, either
one of them fellas could swim the length of Lake Ozonia and back. They
were both good swimmers. But they both drownded in the same river,
one year apart, and pretty near at the same spot."

Migratory pieces like "The Jam on Gerry's Rock" also inspired localized song compositions by area woods singers. Some of these accounts
were creative recastings of older, traditional songs, whereby a songmaker
molded an analogous precedent into topical relevance. Otis Schofell re-
counted the event that inspired "Tebo," a ballad attributed to Roll Grant
and circulated by the A. Sherman Lumber Company, Potsdam, as a
printed text.

> There was a set of falls up there on the Jordan River, maybe a half a mile
> above the Raquette River, where there was a bridge. They called it a "gate
> dam." They'd flood it and put the logs in there, and then they'd open the gate
> and drive the logs on down through into the Raquette at Hollywood.

Well, they was havin' two o'clock lunch there when this fella by the name of Joe Thibault jumped up and clapped his heels together a couple of times. And he said, "The water never run deep enough in the Jordan to drown a man." Two hours later there was a drowned man who lay on the bank of the river, seventy-five or eighty years ago.

Local songmaking among foothills loggers was indicative of the one-time vitality of the heritage as a whole. Clearly not all woods singers were composers, nor were local woodsmen's compositions limited to lumbering subject matter. My findings suggest, however, that most acknowledged "singers" tried their hand at "piecing together" (the customary phrasing) at least one text. The creative impulse was especially pronounced among men with extensive repertories. There was a compulsion to leave one's mark on the tradition, to transform personal experience and response into songs for public sharing.

John Regan of Colton is a case in point. In 1975, at age seventy-eight, he recalled his days entertaining with "The Jam on Gerry's Rock," "Grace Brown and Chester Gillette," "The Wild Colonial Boy," "The Dying Soldier," and "Young Charlotte," among other folk ballads typical of the Northeast-Canadian amalgam. "John was a beautiful singer when he was younger," his wife told me. He gave every indication of retaining that sense of pride during the recitation of a "funny one" of his own making, a personalized adaptation of a Victorian Irish-American ballad, "The Boston Burglar."

THE COLTON BOY

I was born and brought up in Colton, boys, in the place you all know well,
Brought up by honest parents, and the truth to you I'll tell;
Brought up by honest parents and raised most tenderly,
Till I became a roving wreck at the age of twenty-three.

My character it was broken and I was sent to jail;
My parents tried to bail me out but it was of no avail.
A jury found me guilty and the judge he wrote it down;
For the robbing of the Colton bank I was sent to Charlestown.

Now, boys who have your liberty, keep it while you can,
Don't louse around the streets at night to break the laws of man.
For if you do you'll surely rue and turn out just like me,
For I'm serving out my twenty-one years in a penitentiary.

Thus, there was variety within the indigenous song tradition. But foothills loggers were immersed in the occupation that touched their lives daily—whether at home, in camp, or mingling in a barroom. Accordingly, the thrust of their creativity in song reflected an overriding desire to chronicle woods-work events and personalities. Ham Ferry was among the singers who responded to the opportunities.

> Every once in a while you'd get a bunch together here at the inn. It used to be that three or four of us would get together and we'd make up a song. You'd just think of things as they went on. I'd make it up and then we'd keep it goin'. There was quite a few made about the Raquette.
>
> I had one made up about Jim Hickey. He was drownded down near where my father was workin' on the river with him. Down here on Gaine Twist. My father was head boatman and he worked the head all the time—kept the channel open, maybe two or three miles ahead. He didn't work that Sunday; none of them worked unless the river jammed up to where the logs would pile up, and then they'd have to work.
>
> So at Gaine Twist they piled up on a rock. It was all sixteen-foot stuff. They'd keep wedgin' in there on a rock that used to be right out in the middle of the river. Well, Jim Hickey went out to break the jam. They were warpin'. They had ropes they'd hook in and find the key log that was holdin' it. And they'd take the rope back to the rest of the men on the bank and they'd pull on it. He was out to hook the log and started back. He hollered to the boys to pull. And they pulled on it. And the first thing you know, he fell. That was the last they ever saw of him till they found him down the river. The jam broke and he went right on down through with the logs.
>
> I had one on that, and two or three I made up about the Raquette River. But you forget 'em, and now it's hard for me to even start 'em.

Many woods singers, in the Adirondacks and elsewhere, could generally "pick up" appealing song texts and tunes without much difficulty. Often, that meant three or four hearings. Each song, however, presented its own challenges, and as Eddie once put it, some of them "dropped right in place" more easily than others. When surveying the currency of certain material, I became accustomed to hearing remarks to the effect: "I never could get that all together, the whole of it." There was no embarrassment, but sometimes more than a tinge of regret.

Among my various field contacts, Ham Ferry was the most introspective on the matter of memory. The explanation for that, I think, has to do

Adirondack log jam, a hazard for men and a stimulus for songs. Photograph courtesy of the Adirondack Museum.

with Ham's gratefulness for his own inherent and well-exercised powers of recall. Locally, and among peers who are also repositories for much oral lore, Ham's memory is regarded as something of a marvel.

Ham discovered early in life that he could learn appealing material on first or second hearing. "Anything I liked, I could learn it quick," he says. "The next time I heard it, I had it. Just like that. I could pick it up the first time all right. But if I didn't like it, well, I couldn't pick it up. Sometimes I heard a poem. But a poem, if I wrote it over, I could see a picture drawn right on the wall. The second time, I could read it. I could see each line. People say, 'Well, that's stupid.' But that's a fact. I've got it photographed in my mind. Same with the songs."

With advancing age and infrequent singing performances, Ham finds that he has difficulty retrieving all that he has learned. Typical of him, he is almost apologetic about that. Several ballads, nonetheless, remain firmly lodged in his repertory. He attributes that in part to singing them over to himself to relieve monotony—say, when driving—or while in a reflective mood. "Anybody can set there and start broodin' over themselves and things. You know, you get along in life and there's things happenin', and you're wonderin' what's going to happen, and things are gettin' tough to kinda make a livin' at. Well, you get to singin', or you get to recitin' a poem, and you forget about everything else." For Ham, "Utah Carl" is one piece that serves the purpose. He sang it, at my request, at the inn during July, 1970.

UTAH CARL

So you ask me, lit-tle friend, why I'm si-lent, sad and still, Why my
brow is al-ways cloud-y, like the dark-ness on the hill? Run your
po-ny a lit-tle clos-er, and I'll tell you a sim-ple tale Of my
part-ner, U-tah Carl, and his last ride on the trail.

So you ask me, little friend, why I'm silent, sad, and still,
Why my brow is always cloudy, like the darkness on the hill?
Run your pony a little closer, and I'll tell you a simple tale
Of my partner, Utah Carl, and his last ride on the trail.

Out among the cactus and the thistle, in that Mexico fair land,
Where the cattle roam in thousands and in many a bunch and brand,
Now there's a grave without a headstone, without either date nor name;
There is where my partner's lying, there's from a-whence and a-where I
    came.

Long we drove the range together, long we drove them side by side,
And I loved him like a brother, and I wept when Utah died.
Long we drove the range together, cut out, marked the brand,
And when the low sun was setting, joined that night-herd's weary strand.

We were rounding up one morning, when the work was almost done,
On the right the cattle started in their wild and maddened run.
And the boss's little daughter, who was holding on that side,
Started in to turn the cattle, and was there my partner died.

Now, underneath the saddle on the pony which had bore this maid so fair,
Utah Carl that very morning placed a red blanket there.
And there's nothing on the cow range that'll put a cow to flight
Half as quick as some red object, when it's flashed before their sight.

As Lenore rushed her pony to the cattle on the right,
The red blanket slipped beneath her, catching in her stirrups tight.
And Lenore saw her danger, quickly turns her pony's face,
And in leaning from the saddle tries the blanket to displace.

But in leaning from her saddle, the pony gave a bound;
She swept low from her saddle, and she fell upon the ground.
Utah Carl approached the maiden, each foot was sturdy bound;
He swept low from his saddle, at once snatched the girl from harm.

And he rode so fast he passed her, turned and caught her in his arm,
And we thought he was successful, saved from future harm.
But such weight upon those cinches that was never known before;
And those cinches snapped asunder, and he fell beside Lenore.

As Lenore fell from her pony, she had dragged the red blanket down,
And it lay there beside her as she lay upon the ground.
Utah Carl picks up the blanket, "Lie still," he said,
And in running across the prairie waves that blanket over his head.

As he ran across the prairie, every boy gave out a cry;
He had saved the boss's daughter, but they knew that he must die.
He had turned the maddened cattle from Lenore, his little friend,
And the cattle rushed upon him, though he stopped to meet his end.

Quickly from his scabbards Utah Carl his pistols drew:
He was bound to die a-fighting, like a cowboy brave and true.
And his pistols flashed like lightning, and reports rung loud and clear;
Now the herds they were upon him, though he dropped the leading steer.

Now the herds they were upon him, now my partner just had to fall,
Never more to cinch a bronco, never to give a cattle call.

For many singers there is no easy division between song art and song association. "Good" songs, like good poems, fuse memorable form with memorable content. They are expressive links to persons, places, and emotions. Ham Ferry and singers like him responded to that type of fusion in the past, and it does much to explain why some material retains a hold on them in the present. As a youth, for instance, Ham took an immediate liking to the lumbering ballad "Jack Haggerty." Along with "The Jam on Gerry's Rock," he still cites that piece as among his several favorites. Given the Raquette River locale of his home and his father's work, it seems more than coincidental that both songs are about river-driving. Each reflects a thematic tension between the hardship attendant upon the occupation, including separation from women, and the promise of emotional fulfillment and security identified with domestic life. Ham grew up sensitive to the concerns. He sang "Jack Haggerty" one evening at the inn and talked briefly about the song's appeal: "What best sticks out in my mind is that a guy worked all the time and he was thinkin' of coming home to something that wasn't there. Then, afterwards, he tried to get rid of it [i.e., the emotional trauma]. I've known that one ever since I was a kid."

JACK HAGGERTY

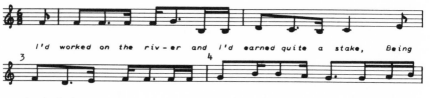

I'd worked on the riv-er and I'd earned quite a stake, Being
stead-fast and stead-y, I had ne'er prov-en the race 'Cause of the

boy that was hap - py, by the bright, whirl - ing stream, And my

thoughts were with Han - nah, and she haunt - ed my dreams.

I'm a broken-down raftsman, from Glenville I came,
And the last words of parting, and the last toils of fame,
For the sharp darts of Cupid, oh, they cause me much grief,
For my heart is asunder, and I can't find relief.

I'd worked on the river and I'd earned quite a stake,
Being steadfast and steady, I had ne'er proven the race
'Cause of the boy that was happy, by the bright, whirling stream,
And my thoughts were with Hannah, and she haunted my dreams.

Now, I'll dress my bride up in the finest of lace,
And the finest of silk herself to embrace;
Now, I gave her my money for me to keep safe;
I denied her of nothing that I have on this earth.

One day on the river, now, a note I received
Saying from her promise herself she'd relieve.
She'd been wed to a young man, not a great while of late,
And the next time I'd see her she would not be a maiden.

Now, it's to her mother I lay all the blame,
She told her forsake me, go back on my name;
For she uncast all rigors for God would soon tied,
And left me to wander till the day that I died.

Now, it's good-bye, Flat River, and the girl I love best,
I'll shoulder my peavey and I will go west;
I'll go to Muskegon, some comfort to find,
And leave my only true love on the Flat River behind.

Now, come all ye good shantyboys with hearts kind and true,
Don't trust any woman, you'll be beat if you do;
And if ever you see one with those dark chestnut curls,
Just think of Jack Haggerty and that Flat River girl.

On several occasions during my visits to Ham's Inn other patrons asked Ham to turn on his jukebox. He usually obliged. The requests were perfectly natural in an age of commercial sound, and Ham is one to please customers. Besides, he says, "there's some good western songs that they play" (i.e., country-western narratives and dramatic recitations set to music). Ham, like Ted and Eddie Ashlaw, has not been immune to the impact of commercial recordings upon foothills song tradition. "Back in the thirties," recalls Eddie, "I'd hear a song on the radio. Hear it once and I could sing it—dropped right in place, the whole song. Time and time again at night I'd be laying down with the radio going and a song would come on. And if I liked the sonofabitch I could sing that song the next day."

Eddie's words often came to mind when I frequented Ham's Inn and places comparable to it. Radios, like jukeboxes, became symptomatic of a trend away from noncommercial, unaccompanied woods singing as interpersonal encounter. Radio entertainment was available in the foothills in the 1920s. The expense and physical size of the early receivers, however, precluded their wide adoption in lumbercamps until the late thirties and early forties. Noted the May, 1940, issue of the *Lumber Camp News*, a monthly report on logging operations and crews from Herkimer County northward: "An increase in the number of radios has been evident this winter. Now practically every camp is equipped with one. Recently several have been installed in bunkhouses."

The prevalence of bunkhouse and barroom performances by lumbermen woods singers declined rapidly after the mid-1950s. Eddie Ashlaw knows well: he was among the last of the active public singers. "Tupper Lake was always pretty good for singing," he told me.

> You'd get in there and the group would be singin', five or six of us and sometimes more [in the Grand Union Hotel]. There was a big crowd come in that liked the singing. And then a bunch would come that were all good singers. We'd get in a huddle at the end of the bar and we'd whoop her up there. I could sing over two hundred songs there one time at Tupper Lake.
>
> We were lumbering up there to Sevey. Went over to the Evergreen Hotel near there every night. By jeez, you'd set there and sing until you went home. This fellow by the name of Cole MacAleese had it. Boy, he liked to hear you sing! Jesus Christ, he would just listen. And, by Jesus, he didn't like it if somebody would go talkin' when you were singing. And he wouldn't be long in tellin' them. Somebody would interrupt a fella while you were singing, and '*Hey!*' [enunciated in a deep, commanding voice in imitation of MacAleese]. He'd ask you to sing and he wanted 'em to listen. I'll never forget it.

Grand Union Hotel at Tupper Lake Junction, N.Y., in 1975. Years earlier, "a bunch would come that were all good singers."

Surely Eddie won't forget that response even though, in his view, Tupper Lake and the Evergreen Hotel and similar "stamping grounds" are "shot to hell now." As he stressed repeatedly during our get-togethers, "They don't sing them old-time songs no more. You start singin' in a bar and they turn the jukebox on." In general that assessment of the foothills heritage is accurate. Yet, as Eddie also knows, "once in a while you'll get in with a few older guys and they want to hear them."

Sometimes those guys aren't so old, and they lug around a tape recorder and camera.

Notes

My approach to the folksong heritage and singers owes much to Alan P. Merriam, *The Anthropology of Music* (Evanston, Ill.: Northwestern University Press, 1964). Merriam argues for consideration of "conceptualization about music, behavior in relation to music, and music sound itself" (p. 32). Treatments reflecting that perspective include three studies by Edward D. Ives, whose influence here will be obvious. See his *Larry Gorman: The Man Who Made the Songs* (Bloomington: Indiana University Press, 1964); *Lawrence Doyle: The Farmer-Poet of Prince Edward Island*, Maine Studies, No. 92 (Orono, Maine: University Press, 1971); and *Joe Scott, the Woodsman-Songmaker* (Urbana: University of Illinois Press, 1978). Additional stimulating works include Roger D. Abrahams, ed., *A Singer and Her Songs: Almeda Riddle's Book of Ballads* (Baton Rouge: Louisiana State University Press, 1970); Henry Glassie, Edward D. Ives, and John F. Szwed, *Folksongs and Their Makers* (Bowling Green, Ohio: Bowling Green University Popular Press, 1970); and Robin Morton, ed., *Come Day, Go Day, God Send Sunday* (London: Routledge and Kegan Paul, 1973). For a groundbreaking study, see Fannie Hardy Eckstorm and Mary Winslow Smyth, *Minstrelsy of Maine: Folk-Songs and Ballads of the Woods and the Coast* (1927; rpt., Ann Arbor, Mich.: Gryphon Books, 1971); contrary to the title's implication, the book contains revealing information about singers and the creative process in a regional folksong tradition.

A number of folksong collections feature material sung by American woodsmen. For the Great Lakes vicinity, see E. C. Beck, *Lore of the Lumber Camps* and *They Knew Paul Bunyan*, as well as Franz Rickaby, *Ballads and Songs of the Shanty-Boy* (Cambridge, Mass.: Harvard University Press, 1926). British and American songs obtained in the Northeast appear in Roland P. Gray, *Songs and Ballads of the Maine Lumberjacks, with Other Songs from Maine* (Cambridge, Mass.: Harvard University Press, 1924); Phillips Barry, ed., *The Maine Woods Songster* (Cambridge, Mass.: Powell Printing Co., 1939); William Main Doerflinger, *Shantymen and Shantyboys: Songs of the Sailor and Lumberman* (New York: Macmillan, 1951); and Horace P. Beck, *The Folklore of Maine* (Philadelphia: J. B. Lippincott, 1957), pp. 245–71. Edith Fowke documents the Ontario heritage in *Lumbering Songs from the Northern Woods*, Publications of the American Folklore Society, Memoir Series, Vol. 55 (Austin: University of Texas Press, 1970), and *Traditional Singers and Songs from Ontario* (Hatboro, Pa.: Folklore Associates, 1965).

For an overview of the variety of songs sung among Northeast and Canadian woodsmen, see Ives, *Joe Scott*, pp. 390–93; Norman Cazden, "Regional and Occupational Orientations of American Traditional Song," *Journal of American Folklore*, 72 (1959), 310–44, correlating material reported from loggers in various regions, including the Catskills; Edith Fowke, "Folk Songs in Ontario," *Canadian Literature*, No. 16 (Spring, 1963), pp. 28–42; and idem, "Anglo-Canadian Folksong: A Survey," *Ethnomusicology*, 16 (1972), 335–50.

With the exception of Thompson's *Body, Boots & Britches*, previous reports of Northern New York folksong tradition among men have excluded the western foothills, concentrating instead upon the eastern Adirondacks and Champlain Valley. Cutting, *Lore of an Adirondack County*, contains thirty song texts (no tunes) from the woods singing tradition in Essex County. For recorded sources with this sectional emphasis, note Milt Okun, *Adirondack Folk Songs and Ballads* (Stinson SLP 82); Pete Seeger, *Champlain Valley Songs* (Folkways FH 5210); Frank Warner, *Frank Warner Sings American Folk Songs and Ballads* (Elektra EKLP-3); and Lawrence Older, *Adirondack Songs, Ballads and Fiddle Tunes* (Folk-Legacy FSA-15). Older is an ex-logger formerly from Saratoga County; Joseph Bruchac III, "Larry Older, Mountain Minstrel," *Adirondack Life*, 5 (Fall, 1974), 30–31, erroneously labels him "the last of the Adirondack minstrels." The other collector-interpreters drew upon songs from the Marjorie Lansing Porter collection of Essex and Clinton county folklore, material as yet largely unpublished. For an idea of Porter's work see her "Collecting Adirondack Folklore," *New York Folklore Quarterly*, 22 (1966), 113–21.

The chapter entitled "Lumbercamp Singing" in Ives, *Joe Scott*, pp. 371–402, contains many findings that parallel my own for the western Adirondack foothills. There are also some interesting differences. The male singers I recorded, for example, employ vocal mannerisms more typically English than the derivative, modestly ornamented, upper-range Irish style found in New Brunswick and among Maritime workers in the Maine woods. For discussion, see Ives, *Joe Scott*, pp. 384–87, and note the field recordings on the one-hour cassette accompanying his book, available separately from the University of Illinois Press.

Ives points out that the *Family Herald* began compiling and printing both songs texts and poetry in 1895, and that the resultant impact on the regional singing tradition deserves further study. See Ives, *Joe Scott*, pp. 103–4, 205–14 *passim*.

In annotating transcribed songs, I refer frequently to index numbers in three standard reference works: for Child ballads, Tristram Potter Coffin, *The British Traditional Ballad in North America*, rev. ed., with a supplement by Roger deV. Renwick (Austin: University of Texas Press, 1977); G. Malcolm Laws, Jr., *Native American Balladry*, rev. ed., Publications of the American Folklore Society, Bibliographical and Special Series, Vol. 1 (1964; rpt., Austin: University of Texas Press, 1975); and idem, *American Balladry from British Broadsides*, Publications of the American Folklore Society, Bibliographical and Special Series, Vol. 8 (Philadelphia: American Folklore Society, 1957). My citations emphasize text and tune currency in the Canadian-American woods singing heritage, and in northeastern North America. This selectivity holds equally for recorded references, which exclude imitative or arranged renditions by nontraditional singers.

"The Lumberjack's Alphabet" is found in Barry, *Maine Woods Songster*, pp. 50–51; Beck, *Lore of the Lumber Camps*, pp. 37–40; Norman Cazden, *A Catskill Songbook* (Fleischmanns, N.Y.: Purple Mountain Press, 1978), pp. 12–13; Eckstorm and Smyth, *Minstrelsy of Maine*, pp. 30–32; Fowke, *Lumbering Songs from the Northern Woods*, pp. 25–27; Gray, *Maine Lumberjacks*, pp. 10–14; Rickaby, *Shanty-Boy*, pp. 35–38; Thompson, *Body, Boots & Britches*, pp. 262–63; Louise Manny and James Reginald Wilson, *Songs of Miramichi* (Fredericton, N.B.: Brunswick Press, 1968), pp. 265–67; and Norman Cazden, "Songs of the Catskills" (manuscript), #3. Recorded versions: *Lumbering Songs from the Ontario Shanties* (Folkways FM 4052), coll. Edith Fowke; *Songs of the Michigan Lumberjacks* (Library of Congress AAFS L56), ed. E. C. Beck; Sara Cleveland, *Sara Cleveland* (Philo 1020).

For discussion of songs similar to "Cousin Nellie," see Ives, *Joe Scott*, pp. 391–92, and Edith Fowke, "A Sampling of Bawdy Ballads from Ontario," in

Folklore & Society: Essays in Honor of Benj. A. Botkin, ed. Bruce Jackson (Hatboro, Pa.: Folklore Associates, 1966), pp. 45–61. The tune for "Cousin Nellie" is the same one Ted Ashlaw uses for "When the Work's All Done This Fall" (Laws B3). See also Cazden, "Songs of the Catskills," #154 ("The Barefoot Boy").

Tupper Lake barrooms were favorites among loggers who enjoyed traditional music. Stewart H. Holbrook, *Yankee Loggers: A Recollection of Woodsmen, Cooks, and River Drivers* (New York: International Paper Co., 1961), notes that "the American House, the Canadian Hotel (Joe Gokey's place), the Iroquois, the Altamount, and Dave Denise's Saloon, together with lesser places and the Faust Hotel [later, the Grand Union Hotel] at the Junction presented practically unlimited possibilities for entertainment" (p. 60).

"The Jam on Gerry's Rock" (Laws C1) is an archetypal lumbering ballad, with innumerable variants in print; Ted Ashlaw's text and tune are the common ones. For representative examples, see Barry, *Maine Woods Songster*, pp. 52–53; Beck, *Lore of the Lumber Camps*, pp. 194–97; Cazden, *Catskill Songbook*, pp. 6–7; Eckstorm and Smyth, *Minstrelsy of Maine*, pp. 82–90; Fowke, *Lumbering Songs from the Northern Woods*, pp. 95–99; Gray, *Maine Lumberjacks*, pp. 3–9; Manny and Wilson, *Songs of Miramichi*, pp. 115–17; Rickaby, *Shanty-Boy*, pp. 11–19; Thompson, *Body, Boots & Britches*, pp. 259–60. Recorded versions: Tom Brandon, *"The Rambling Irishman": Tom Brandon of Peterborough, Ontario* (Folk-Legacy FSC-10); Marie Hare, *Marie Hare of Strathadam, New Brunswick* (Folk-Legacy FSC-9); *Lumbering Songs from the Ontario Shanties; Songs of the Michigan Lumberjacks*. The geographical location of "Gerry's Rock" is uncertain; cases have been made for rivers in Maine, Michigan, and Canada. My contacts opted for Canadian origin on the basis of local hearsay and textual wording.

"Tebo" (Laws C6), briefly mentioned, is found without tune in the *Box Mark*, 2:10 (Mar., 1926); I located a copy of that publication at the Adirondack Museum archives. Texts also appear in Thompson, *Body, Boots & Britches*, pp. 275–77, and Cutting, *Lore of an Adirondack County*, pp. 18–19. For "The Colton Boy," see references for "The Boston Burglar" (Laws L16 B).

"Utah Carl" (Laws B4) is common in collections of cowboy folksongs: for instance, John A. Lomax and Alan Lomax, *Cowboy Songs and Other Frontier Ballads*, rev. and enl. ed. (New York: Macmillan Co., 1948), p. 125, and Glenn Ohrlin, *The Hell-Bound Train: A Cowboy Songbook* (Urbana: University of Illinois Press, 1973), pp. 153–55. Recorded versions: see Harlan Daniel's discography in Ohrlin, *Hell-Bound Train*, p. 273; and *Sara Cleveland*, an album by a Champlain valley traditional singer.

Kenneth S. Goldstein has explored the question of song appeal; see "On the Application of the Concepts of Active and Inactive Traditions to the Study of Repertory," in *Toward New Perspectives in Folklore*, ed. Américo Paredes and Richard Bauman, Publications of the American Folklore Society, Bibliographical and Special Series, Vol. 23 (Austin: University of Texas Press, 1972), pp. 62–67. "Some songs," Goldstein observes, "which might otherwise be expected to become part of inactive repertory because of their topical nature or their identification with a specific group, will continue to remain part of the permanent repertory because of special esthetic appeal they may have for the singer" (pp. 64–65).

"Jack Haggerty" (Laws C25) was composed by a logger at Flat River, Michigan, in 1872; the people were real, but the events fictional. Laws, *Native American Balladry*, pp. 58–59, discusses the ballad's origin. For variants see Barry, *Maine Woods Songster*, pp. 74–75; Beck, *Lore of the Lumber Camps*, pp. 140–48; Cazden, "Songs of the Catskills," #6; Eckstorm and Smyth, *Minstrelsy of Maine*, pp. 124–26; Fowke, *Lumbering Songs from the Northern Woods*, pp. 187–89; Rickaby, *Shanty-Boy*, pp. 3–10. Recorded versions: Brandon, *"Rambling Irishman"*; *Lumbering Songs from the Ontario Shanties*; *Songs of the Michigan Lumberjacks*.

Notice of the radios in foothills lumbercamps appeared in *Lumber Camp News*, 2:1 (May, 1940), 3. Prior to 1940, the infrequent sets were usually acquired through donation rather than lumber company purchase.

On the expectation of audience silence and attentiveness during a solo singer's performance, see also Ives, *Joe Scott*, p. 383. Ives links this to the coaxing pattern that holds as well for the Adirondack heritage.

6

The Roving Ashlaw Man

Eddie Ashlaw says he has always made a point of "getting around." Few people who know Eddie would challenge the claim, and it is a lifestyle that shaped his active years as a foothills lumberman and public entertainer. "He knew a lot more of the guys than I did," observes his younger brother Ted. "There was no limit to them. No matter where he went he always knew somebody." For Eddie, that peer socializing often has gone hand in hand with drink and song. In his words, "It ain't too many years ago in the gin mills there'd be singing, a lot of singing. I'd hardly go out drinking and there'd be somebody wants me to sing. If you're feeling good, why, then you do it."

Folklore fieldworkers quickly learn the value of leads furnished by others. Such was the case one evening at Ham's Inn in the summer of 1970. Ham and I were talking about the "old songs." He reiterated that he was familiar with the material, but felt most comfortable reminiscing about other woodsmen-singers. "Eddie Ashlaw used to know them songs, and I've heard *him* sing them. He used to know quite a few of those." Later I met Eddie's middle-aged nephew in a chance encounter at the establishment. He confirmed that Eddie had a repertory of "many old-time songs that nobody has recorded yet." Both men had witnessed Eddie singing in several hotel barrooms and taverns, Ham's Inn among them. He was the kind of man I wanted to find.

It wasn't long before I was standing at the door of Eddie's roadside dwelling near Parishville Center. Rain was falling and it was nearing dusk. My visit was unannounced, for he had no telephone. I knocked tentatively. There was a stir and an immediate friendly greeting. "Come on in!" a voice boomed. "The door's open." I had aroused Eddie from a nap.

80

Eddie Ashlaw at home. Parishville Center, N.Y., August, 1974.

He was groggy as we came face to face—a burly, heavy-jowled woods-man who at age sixty-nine appeared younger than his years.

I briefly explained my presence and the cassette tape recorder clutched in one hand. Eddie understood. He moved toward a refrigerator and of-fered me a beer, apologizing for his unkempt state. He had earlier re-turned from several barrooms and had hoped to get some rest before fix-ing dinner. A shuffleboard game, tables and chairs, and numerous small appliances were stacked in disarray around an otherwise barren room. I could see a cot behind a partition at one end. Eddie noted that the place had been run as a small restaurant, but the operation had folded and he had moved in. The quarters were adequate, he said, for a man living alone.

The living conditions had become more rustic when I returned to see him in late December of that year. Again I arrived to find that he had been napping after a round of social drinking. Again, too, he greeted me with the kind of cordiality one associates with old friends rather than brief acquaintances. This time snow was falling and it was bitter cold.

We retired to the back portion of the structure, where Eddie had sealed off a room with transparent plastic sheeting. The quarters were cramped: his bed, refrigerator, and stove left little space for movement. The oven door was open, with the stove's four burners turned on to maximum. The heat was incredible. Eddie sat down on the edge of his cot. Dressed in well-worn woodsmen's long johns, he presented a striking figure as he recalled "the old days in Tupper when money was like nothing," an era when he could "set and sing all night."

Eddie was born in 1901 near Lake Ozonia, a short distance from Hopkinton at the east-central border of St. Lawrence County. He is the third oldest of five brothers and three sisters. His grandparents were French-Canadian. Eddie spent his youth on the small family farm and in the lumber woods, around St. Regis Falls, with his parents. He attended a local one-room school through eighth grade before leaving home at the age of thirteen. The departure marked the beginning of a forty-year career as a western Adirondack logger.

By Eddie's accounting, between the years 1914 and 1955 he worked for "pretty near everybody" from St. Regis Falls to Tupper Lake, and south to Utica. Prior to 1920 he found jobs on St. Regis Paper Company lands near his home and drove river on the Indian, Red, and Moose waters in Herkimer and Lewis counties, to the south. Thereafter, he joined up with Ted. Among other places, the brothers worked on operations at Woods Lake, Loon Lake, and Limekiln Lake under management of the Gould and International paper companies. During the 1923–24 season, at the age of twenty-two, Eddie was among the first of the men to sign on for a major clearing operation along the Beaver River. He was later to chronicle some of the ensuing events in song. Says Ted, "Eddie and Levi [a brother] worked peelin' pulp. There was never no man that ever went through the Adirondacks that could begin to follow those two barksmen. They could take the bark off a tree faster than anything we ever saw." A job at Brandreth, along the upper reaches of the Beaver River, rounded off the decade.

Eddie returned to the vicinity of St. Regis Falls and Tupper Lake about 1930. He once again found employment with the St. Regis Paper Company, this time at Bay Pond. After a season or two he shifted to cutting operations managed by the Oval Wood Dish Company. The Depression interrupted the pattern. The local lumber industry was hard hit, and Eddie spent 1937–38 working in Buffalo on dock construction for the Bethlehem Steel Corporation. Conditions improved the following year. He returned to the North Country and took to jobbing by the cord for Sisson and White, a Potsdam-based firm with timber tracts near Childwold.

His reputation and crews had begun to expand by the early 1940s, a role significant enough to warrant military exemption. One of Eddie's larger camps averaged between seventy-five and eighty men over an eleven-year period. According to Ted, Eddie had two hundred men working for him by the conclusion of World War II. Reports on the operations appeared in the *Lumber Camp News* from July, 1941, to August, 1945, and confirm the oral accounts. A *News* item of 1942, for example, specified that Eddie's crew had cut 2,000,000 board feet of hardwood during the season, and 2,000 cords of pulp. That success led to profound changes in the life of the self-described "poor boy."

The years 1945 through 1955 were a boom period for Eddie Ashlaw. People in the area still speak of the great "blowdown" on November 25, 1950, during which high winds leveled countless trees in the western and southern Adirondacks. Eddie remembers that "she took everything down for miles. You could walk right on trees with a cord and a half, two cords in them." The clearing work was difficult but profitable for those jobbers, like Eddie, who had extensive financial backing, equipment, and luck. He flourished for several years, with the notable exception of 1951. "I lost about $35,000 there at Jerseyfield," he told me. "Rained all winter and couldn't get a goddamn thing out." It was a major setback, yet Eddie had recovered from them before. "As Joe Pruff used to say," Ted recalled once, " 'That fella, take and strip his pockets, and bury him naked in a pile of stones, and he'll crawl out. And when he gets out he'll have a new suit and have his pockets full of money.' No matter what happened, Eddie always could come back." And so it was through the mid-1950s.

Eddie began to spend and drink freely. "He was one for big blowouts," I was told. "He liked to spend it, and he did. He knew everybody and his brother." Gradually he turned away from his direct involvement in woods work. For a brief time he operated a boardinghouse for loggers at Hollywood, on the Raquette. It burned, and in 1955 he purchased the Grand Union Hotel at Tupper Lake Junction. "When I bought it," he says, "Tupper Lake was still jumpin' pretty good. Lots of money. Christ, there was thousands and thousands of lumberjacks coming in with their money."

The Grand Union Hotel continued under Eddie's management until 1962. It turned out to be a bad investment. After 1955 the state closed access to forest preserve lands opened for blowdown salvage. The labor force dwindled as local men sought work elsewhere or at other trades. Profits in the hotel's barroom began to plummet, a situation compounded by Eddie's generosity in extending loans and buying drinks. To make matters worse, at one point two deserters from the Canadian army stole one of the checkbooks with which Eddie paid his crew and bought equipment. "They got around $7,000 to $8,000," he says with bitterness. Eddie was insured for the loss. The incident, however, seems to have marked a turning point in his career. He sold the hotel and much of his considerable real estate.

Eddie avoided talking about the intervening years between 1962 and 1970. My impression is that they were ones of considerable readjustment and maybe a bit painful. Certainly things had changed a great deal by the time I met him. Eddie's thoughts were of other times and those people who knew or still remembered him for assertive independence and good-naturedness. He has always been one to seize opportunity, to take life on his own terms. Witness his explanation for selling the hotel and real estate: "I just decided to get the hell out," he stresses, "so I did. I live for today, for the minute. It didn't mean a thing to me, places or camps or houses or anything. When I was ready to move I'd just do it." This philosophy has been central to Eddie's activities and feelings as a woods singer; it also affected my experiences in documenting his repertory of songs.

Eddie's initial exposure to what he terms "old-time songs" came at home and in the woods. In his youth he picked up texts and tunes from a close neighbor named Johnny Pelow, a highly admired traditional singer who also influenced Ted, Wilfred Monica, and undoubtedly other woods singers. Once engaged in woods work, Eddie had contact with comparable artists. Among them was Johnny Killen, from whom he learned "The Wild Mustard River." The ballad is representative of the "river songs" (Eddie's subcategory) performed while on the Beaver and Moose River jobs in the twenties. I recorded Eddie's version in the fall of 1975.

THE WILD MUSTARD RIVER

Come all of you boys of the riv-er, Pay at-ten-tion to me for a-while, I will sing you a song of the sad fate Be-fell my friend, chum, John-ny Stile.

Come all of you boys of the river,
Pay attention to me for a while,
I will sing you a song of the sad fate
Befell my friend, chum, Johnny Stile.

We were camped on the Wild Mustard River,
It's down by the old Henry Dam.
As we rolled from our blankets one morning
On the rocks there we spied a big jam.

It's then we got up and got ready
With peaveys and picks we supplied,
While some of the boys took the foot trail
To open the reservoir dam.

For the waters came rushing and roaring
Right down on the tail-end of the jam,
For you know how the waters wild flowing
With a flood from a reservoir dam.

For we worked for an hour and a quarter,
We had worked till hauling it seemed most despair,
But after the waters got worked all through her,
Like lightning she pulled out of there.

It's "Ride her, ride down to dead waters,"
Our foreman he cried, we obeyed.
Not a man in our number but had rode her,
Not a man in our crew was afraid.

There was not a man on the logs better
Than my friend, it's my chum, Johnny Stile,
For he'd rode in her more times than any,
But always was careless and wild.

This day luck had proved hard against him:
His foot, it got caught in the jam.
And you know how the waters wild flowing,
They roll in but they never roll out.

For we'd worked for an hour and a quarter,
We had worked till the sweat down did pour,
And when that we'd got his poor body
It did not look like him any more.

He was crushed from his feet to his shoulders,
He was rolled out as thin as your hand;
But he never squealed till it was all over,
For Johnny had plenty of sand.

We buried him beneath the green willows,
Where the larks and the nightingales sing,
His grave it was covered with flowers,
Wild flowers that bloom in the spring.

Way down on the Wild Mustard River,
Poor Johnny lies under the sod,
For on earth we'll find rest for his body
And hope that his soul is with God.

Eddie also learned some "western songs," cowboy-inspired material that seems to have been more prevalent among English-speaking Adirondack and Ontario loggers than among their Maine and Maritime counterparts. Greater access to early American-issue commercial recordings of cowboy ballads, and to radio stations promoting such records, may help account for the difference. "Catch somebody who could sing," Eddie explains, "well, they had different songs. There was a guy who went west. When he came back he knew five or six songs we hadn't heard." Among them was "The Tenderfoot":

THE TENDERFOOT

One Spring I thought I'd have some fun, I'd learn how punch-ing cows were done, And when the round-up had be-gun, I'd tack-le the cat-tle king; Said he, "My fore-man, he's in town, he's in the sa-loon and his name is Brown; I think that we can

take him down." Said I, "That's just the thing."

One spring I thought I'd have some fun,
I'd learn how punching cows were done,
And when the roundup had begun,
I'd tackle the cattle king;
Said he, "My foreman, he's in town,
He's in the saloon and his name is Brown;
I think that we can take him down."
Said I, "That's just the thing."

Next day we started for the ranch,
Brown talked to me 'most all the way,
For he says punching cows was nothing but play,
That it wasn't no work at all;
"For all you have to do is ride,
It's just like drifting o'er the tide."
And jiminy jiminy, how he lied;
He surely had his gall.

For he put me in charge of the cavyyard,
Said, "Now, my boy, don't work too hard.
For all that you have to do is guard
Those horses from getting away."
He had two hundred and sixty head,
And ofttimes wished that I was dead;
When one of those horses would get away,
Brown's face it would turn red,
And this is the truth, I say.

When one of those horses would get away
It was just like running for a stake,
For sometimes you could not head them at all,
And other times my horse would fall,

And I'd shoot on like a cannonball
Till the earth came in my way.

For next they saddled me up an old gray hack
With a great big setfast on his back,
And they padded him up with gunny sacks;
They used my bedding and all.
When I got on he quit the ground,
He went in the air and he turned around.
When I came down I busted the ground—
That was a scandalous fall.

For they picked me up and brought me in,
They rolled me down with a rolling pin.
"For that is the way we all begin,
You're doing well," said Brown.
"And in the morning if you don't die,
Another horse I'll let you try."
"Oh, won't you let me walk?" said I,
"Or I'll go back to town."

Oh, I've traveled up and I've wandered down,
I've traveled this wide world round and round,
I've lived in cities and lived in town,
But I have this much to say:
Before you go west go kiss your wife,
Get a heavy insurance upon your life,
And gut yourself with a butcher knife,
You'll find it the easiest way!

It became clear in our first talk that Eddie had a well-developed sense of his image and ability as a bunkhouse and barroom singer. Although aging, he refuses to compromise his high standards of vocal quality and the importance of "getting the air [i.e., tune] right." As he once put it, "I know when I'm singing, and when I can't." I asked Eddie how he knew when he was performing up to the personal criteria. "I just feel like it," he replied. "It just comes right out of me, easy. Sometimes I get feelin' just right and the songs will flow right out. Your voice varies a lot. There's sometimes I wouldn't sing for nobody; it's different from those professional singers who practice and sing all the time."

Singing, for Eddie, has been tied up with self-esteem. I quickly learned that he sings when he wants to sing; unlike his brother and several other contacts, Eddie was much less responsive to prompting in an interview situation. He insists on having things on his own terms. In time I came to realize just how important the right mood, the right crowd, and the right place have been in shaping his activities as a traditional performer.

From the outset, Eddie talked about his songs and singing in terms of situations and people he has known. For example, when I asked him what types of songs he liked, he answered, "Ah, I like most any songs. Yah, we used to get drunk. I'll tell you, we used to sing quite a bit. Used to sing a lot of Irish songs with Steve Hurley. He was a good singer; he died in 1969. Most all the songs he sang were on records." On another occasion I asked Eddie if he was accustomed to singing special songs for certain people. He replied, "Well, ordinarily, if you knew 'em you'd sing what they asked for, what they wanted to hear. It's just like that Junior Francis. He likes that song 'Don't Say Goodbye If You Must Go.' Three or four verses, about all. It's a good song. It hits him. Yeah, he's a guy who likes to hear a good singer." The more I asked about such situations, the more a pattern emerged: for Eddie, singing and socializing were inseparable, and social drinking among friends provided the natural occasion and stimulus. An exchange we had in December, 1970, brought the pattern into focus.

Eddie: "I was in the VFW in Potsdam a while ago. First time I had ever been in there. Somebody tried singin'. The guy that was with me knew that I knew quite a few old-timers. Christ, I was singin' in there for over three hours, I guess. I sang that 'Jam on Gerry's Rock'—and Jesus Christ, they wondered if I ever knew that. Christly old-time songs."

RDB: "Well, anytime you feel like singing, just let me know. I'd love to hear you sing those 'old-time songs.'"

Eddie: "You just find a few people. The guy in Nicholville, Junior Francis, he could sit and listen to you sing all day. I go fishing with him. Stop for a beer and drinks. Wherever we're drinking, he wants you to sing."

The pattern helped explain why time and again, when I stopped to talk with Eddie, he was reluctant to sing. I grew to expect his pat response to my requests for songs: "I ain't in no mood for singing *today!*" In Eddie's case, at least, the pattern went beyond the usual coaxing expectation among woods singers. At one point, half in frustration and half in jest, I suggested that I might bring a bottle along on the next visit. "No," he said, "I hardly ever drink at home." It was Eddie's way of saying that the alcohol was but one of the necessary ingredients; an artificial environment was just that, no matter how much I would wish it were otherwise.

It dawned on me that I had fallen prey to the lure of his repertory. In trying to induce Eddie to sing on my terms, I was asking him to violate a norm basic to his personal woods singing. There was good reason for his reticence. "I never sung for drinks," he continued. "If I wanted a drink I bought it. If somebody wanted me to sing for them I sang. I didn't have to sing for drinks; I sung because I *wanted* to sing. Years ago that was the big deal."

In many ways, singing the old songs remains a "big deal" for Eddie Ashlaw, especially in recent years as the opportunities have become more infrequent. The songs he once sang in bunkhouses and barrooms became an important part of the man and his public identity. Knowing them brought status and esteem, and time and change have made him extremely possessive about that repertory.

Eddie, in short, is not the kind of singer to share his material casually with a stranger, particularly one with a tape recorder. That most of his songs are in public domain is of little matter. As far as Eddie is concerned, pieces like "The Wild Mustard River" and "The Tenderfoot" are rightfully his by interpersonal inheritance and default. And as different as the two ballads are in spirit, both are commentaries on the trials and tribulations of virile work. Together, they suggest part of the intricate mesh of Eddie's personality, work experience, and song repertory. He learned those two songs from a friend. Says Eddie, "I've never heard nobody else that ever could sing 'em. He'd dead, so I *know* there's nobody knows 'em. So that's it."

My periodic interviews with Eddie spanned five years. For the first three of those years he stuck by his resolve, declining to sing more than fragments of songs. He sensed my growing frustration. We both knew that he could perform. What was worse, I began to suspect that he rather enjoyed my predicament. It became our private game, to the point that he once consented to sing on a subsequent occasion provided there was no tape recorder: he would search me at the door. That was a fine jest. He rubbed it in by labeling me a "sing-picker."

The major breakthrough came on an August afternoon in 1974. I had driven from my temporary field residence at Sterling Pond to Parishville Center in hopes of finding Eddie at home. Often before, those treks had proven unsuccessful. But this time luck was with me. My car passed his blue pickup truck about a mile from my destination. Suspecting that he might be headed for a nearby tavern, I wheeled around and followed in pursuit. To this day I don't know if he noticed me in his rear-view mirror (I would like to believe that he didn't). We ended up at the Timber Tavern on the outskirts of Parishville. Greetings were exchanged and he invited

me to join him for a drink. I was prepared with questions. Eddie had
come to expect them, especially the ones about a song entitled "Bush
LaPorte." He asked if I had a miniature tape recorder in my pocket. I
assured him that my equipment was in the car. Satisfied, he took a swallow of beer and sang. It was the outset of a new stage in our rapport.

Of the ten songs that Eddie singled out during our first get-together,
none was more intriguing than "Bush LaPorte" (alternately entitled "I'm
Just a Common Lumberhick"). I had brought along a copy of Edith
Fowke's excellent Canadian collection *Lumbering Songs from the Northern Woods*. Eddie recognized several of the pieces as we leafed through
the contents. Suddenly he looked up at me.

> I know some old ones that ain't in that book. They ain't got the song I made
> up in there. It's a woods song about old Creighton, Sisson and White, Sullivan
> here to Colton, Jerry Hayes—they're all in the thing. Bush LaPorte, he lum-
> bered. He played fiddle. That's all he cared about, his fiddle. He'd dead now.
> Yup, he's the one that started that song we made up. They were so cheap in
> their wages at Oval Wood Dish. We had 'em *all* in there, I'll tell ya. It was just
> what you went through: work in one place and what you had to put up with—
> the lice and all that. "I'm Just a Common Lumberhick." That's all we ever
> named that one. Most of 'em called it "Bush LaPorte" because it started with
> him. I and a buddy made it up about the woods as we worked through our old
> camps.

Eddie sang the first two stanzas and stopped. "That lumberjack song,
I wouldn't even sing it to you. That's not recorded nowhere. And I
wouldn't have it on, either, because nobody else knows it. Only me." Did
he mean that other singers deferred to him because of his role in the composition process? "That ain't the idea," Eddie continued. "It's quite a
long song and they've never got it all together right. They can never sing
it. They can try it but they never get it. That's what I mean." He wasn't
about to risk altering that situation in the summer of 1970. And so it
went until the summer of 1974 and the Timber Tavern rendition. A year
later he consented to put "I'm Just a Common Lumberhick" on tape.

I'M JUST A COMMON LUMBERHICK
(BUSH LAPORTE)

I'm just a com-mon lum-ber-hick, and I've made a pile of jack,   I

I'm just a common lumberhick, and I've made a pile of jack,
I shot the wad, and now, by God, I won't try to have it back;
I haven't a pain, so I can't complain, but a few things I will mention,
I won't be long in singing my song, if you'll give me your attention.

Well, the first time I went in the woods, boys, I wished that I was dead,
I got in with a bunch of "Frogs" and a dirty, lousy bed.
Well, the pusher's name was Bush LaPorte, he weren't a bad sorter of log;
You'd always see him smoking his pipe, and patting the head of his dog.

When told at the camp that the ice was gone and a pair of his horses were in,
He said not a word but he kept right on a-playing his old violin.
But this winter was finally over, boys, and at last the logs were in;
We bade good-bye to Bush LaPorte, his dog, and his old violin.

Then I went to Beaver River, it's a place just up the line;
I didn't save much money, but I had a hell of a time.
I cleaned land by the acre till the fire burnt my shoes,
I shot the wad in poker chips, and had quite a few bottles of booze.

But it couldn't last forever, boys, it finally went on the hog,
Then I had to hunt for another place, well, another place to log.
Then I went down on the lousy line—I made good money, too;
I liked the work, and I liked the place, and I liked the whole damn crew.

Old Kelly kept the wages up as long as he held sway;
But old Creighton cut them all to hell when Kelly got out of his way.

Then I went in for the Oval Dish, nicknamed by some "The Plate,"
And when the wages are in style those people are up to date.
Old Creighton set the wages, and he set them mighty small,
For all he paid was a dollar a day, and we had to hit the ball.

Then I went down for Sisson and White—I think it was the worst of all;
But what could I do in my summer clothes when the time was late in the fall?
Jim Sullivan was the pusher there, with his assistant, Jerry Hayes;
Of all the pushers you ever saw they certainly had queer ways.

Jim Sullivan was the pusher there, he's a grouchy son-of-a-gun,
If his Indians would ever turn on him he'd certainly have some fun!
But this winter was finally over, boys, and I certainly felt glad;
But I had to stay in work for small pay, and I sure felt mighty bad.

For I've worked through this woods, boys, I've worked up and down the
     line,
I've worked in spruce and balsam, and I've taken my turn in pine.
But I've come to this conclusion, and I'll stick to it evermore:
If your boy wants to go to the woods next fall, shoot him the spring before.

All the evidence indicates that "Bush LaPorte" is a chronicle of actual logging experience. I am convinced that the depiction is valid auto-biography, albeit highly selective. "Bush LaPorte" is an account bent through the prism of personal impression and opinion. Whether or not the point of view is wholly Eddie's is more difficult to determine. Pressed on the authorship issue, Eddie admits that a co-worker named Elmer Jones helped put the song together. Conceivably he was the principal au-thor. Ted Ashlaw recalls that Jones "wrote out" the song in longhand during the composition process "back in the Depression." It is more likely, however, that "Bush LaPorte" was a product of joint effort, wherein the two men pooled their collective experience and views but settled on a first-person point of view. That way, the "I" of the lyrics would serve either singer in performance.

"I'm Just a Common Lumberhick" announces itself as flashback public testimony to self, work, and personal philosophy. Surely there is a great deal of Eddie Ashlaw projected through the sentiment. The first stanza introduces the rags-to-riches pattern, the reversal of fortune, and the ever-present sense of pride and self-esteem. The second couplet hints that the song is designed for intoxicated singing among in-group peers. In short, anyone who knew Eddie would immediately identify the singer with the song. They would be prepared for some of the uncompromising reflections to follow.

According to Eddie, the events pick up in 1918–19 on a job for the St. Regis Paper Company. There were many French-Canadians ("Frogs") in the crew, and the juxtaposition of them with the "dirty, lousy bed" is far from accidental. Here, as in other instances, discussion with a living songmaker proved invaluable. "They were a dirty bunch, them first ones that come in," Eddie explained. "They'd wash their socks right in the washing dish there to Bush LaPorte's, and rinse their toothbrush right in the same water." Arthur "Bush" LaPorte, well known as a lumber jobber in the Tupper Lake area, was memorable for other reasons. As Wilfred Monica put it, Bush was a highly admired woods boss, "a slow, easy-going fella and an excellent step-dancer who loved to fiddle."

The fourth stanza leaps to 1923–24 and the Beaver River operation near Limekiln. The work entailed clearing 47,000 acres of timber for the Stillwater Reservoir project. Recalled Ted, "They wanted the logs and they wanted the pulp. Everything that was left had to be burned. Eddie was twenty-two; I was eighteen." Several contacts noted that Eddie supplemented his wages with illicit liquor sales.

When I first mentioned the song to Ted, he immediately recited the sixth stanza with obvious enjoyment. "There was a lot of truth to it," he explained several years later. "When Kelly got done for the St. Regis Paper Company, then Creighton cut the wages. It was back in 1931. The St. Regis company just went dead. It went right out. He couldn't cut them too much as long as the paper company was going." The Oval Wood Dish Company absorbed the smaller firm, a victim of the early Depression. In all likelihood, then, Thomas Creighton's wage policy was a justified crisis measure. But management and labor do not always see eye to eye on such measures. The sixth and seventh stanzas come across as unmitigated resentment and censure. I asked Eddie how prominent lumbermen like Creighton felt about that type of biting cynicism circulated in song. Would there be reprisals? Eddie's reply took me by surprise.

"If it was the truth, they'd take it. If they fit, well, that was it. When we figured it was the truth we sang it to ya. And we never picked out who the

"I liked the work, and I liked the place, and I liked the whole damn crew. . . ." Although it presents a different lumber crew than that mentioned in "Bush LaPorte," Eddie Ashlaw identifies closely with this 1930s group portrait. Photograph courtesy of Edward Ashlaw.

hell was listening. It's just like when I was singing that 'Bush LaPorte' song. We ain't rubbin' that Oval Wood Dish very nice. And I've sung it right to him—old Creighton—in the bar that used to be across from the Municipal Park in Tupper Lake."

Such songs, among woodsmen, were understood in context for what they were: impressionistic vignettes that assumed esoteric knowledge. It was up to each listener to weigh the details against experience, to discriminate between defensible gripes and good-natured ribbing. The final stanzas of "Bush LaPorte," like all those preceding, take for granted this kind of knowledgeable audience. Sullivan and Hayes in actuality served in the capacities indicated. But both men were popular favorites among local loggers, including Eddie, and hence targets for jibes without malicious intent. To know that is to know "Bush LaPorte" as an insider.

The textual evidence of "I'm Just a Common Lumberhick" suggests that it was composed no later than 1940. During that year James Sullivan moved on to a pulpwood job at Long Pond, whereas Eddie's song refers to Sullivan's 1939 work for Sisson and White at Usher Farm, Childwold. Jerry Hayes died in 1941, Sullivan in 1945. The concluding two stanzas hint that the singer-songmaker has reached a transition point in occupational experience. Eddie Ashlaw in 1940 had reached that point. He had cause to reflect, through song, on his past. The humorous sarcasm owed much to "The Tenderfoot" (most obvious in stanza 10). By 1940, Eddie was the kind of self-assured and contented lumberman who could enjoy the whims of occupational initiation.

Although Eddie's woods work is well behind him nowadays, he has no intention of forgetting songs like "The Tenderfoot" and "Bush LaPorte." Too much of his life has been bound up in the pieces and too many memories in the singing. "Every once in a while I'll ride along," he explained,

> and one will come back to me that I haven't thought of in years. I know a lot of songs yet. Christ, I could sing for a week. Them that I kinda hate to forget, I tune them over once in a while just to remember them.
>
> I'd like to get in with some buggers who enjoy singing. But you don't see too much of that no more. You just don't. Once in a while I meet a few of the boys that used to work for me. They want me to sing that lumberjack song [i.e., "Bush LaPorte"] pretty near every time. So, if we decide we're going to sing, I sing. I don't stop. I figure I've spent enough money at the bars that I'm entitled to my place there. They ain't going to put me away, either. So that's the way it goes. But they don't sing like they used to.

When I last spoke with Eddie, he seemed more resolved than ever not to let anything, or anyone, get the best of him. He was bringing in earnings doing carpentry work, and he had moved into a comfortable although modest mobile home down the road from where I first met him. He left little doubt in my mind that he had adjusted happily to his postlogging circumstances. The songs and the singing talent remained archways to the past and to the people who had known him at the zenith of his career. He once said it all in one sentence: "I've had my fling and I flung it—I spent it while I had it, and I don't have any regrets." That indomitable spirit comes across in a reworked British traditional song that Eddie "made over once, and the boys all got a charge out of it in Tupper Lake." His title for the autobiographical composition is fitting: "The Roving Ashlaw Man."

THE ROVING ASHLAW MAN

I am that roving Ashlaw man, and I've roamed from town to town,
If liquor don't give you the answer, boys, come on here, won't you sit down?
With tackle on my shoulder and my peavey in my hand,
When I reach St. Regis Falls, I'll be a healthy young Ashlaw man.

Well, when I first came to Tupper Lake, the girls all jumped with joy,
Said one unto the other, "Here comes that Ashlaw boy!"
One treats me to a bottle, while the other to a dram,
And the toast went round the table: "Here's to that healthy Eddie Ashlaw
   man."

For I hadn't been in Tupper Lake for a day not only three,
When Papin's lovely daughter, she fell in love with me.
She said she wanted to marry me, and takes me by the hand,
And she went home and told her mother that she loved that Ashlaw man.

Notes

"The Wild Mustard River" (Laws C5) is found in Beck, *Lore of the Lumber Camps*, pp. 202–6; Fowke, *Lumbering Songs from the Northern Woods*, pp. 107–10; Manny and Wilson, *Songs of Miramichi*, pp. 306–7. Recorded versions:

Lumbering Songs from the Ontario Shanties; Songs of the Michigan Lumberjacks. Eddie's tune is the one commonly found with this text.

"The Tenderfoot" (Laws B27) was composed by cowboy-poet Dominick J. O'Malley in 1893 under the title "The 'D2' Horse Wrangler," and published by him under a pseudonym in the *Stock Growers' Journal*, Miles City, Montana, on February 3, 1894. For full details see John I. White, *Git Along, Little Dogies: Songs and Songmakers of the American West* (Urbana: University of Illinois Press, 1975), pp. 73–100; the ballad appears on pp. 89–91. The word "cavyyard" in the third stanza is a corruption of the Spanish *caballada*, meaning a herd of horses. A "setfast" is a saddle sore. Eddie uses the familiar tune, although his handling of it in the recorded performance is unusual.

Reed, *Lumberjack Sky Pilot*, pp. 55–95 *passim*, contains references to lumbering operations and personnel mentioned in "I'm Just a Common Lumberhick." See Cazden, "Songs of the Catskills," #108, for a piece ("Puttin' On the Style") with the same tune.

"The Roving Ashlaw Man" is based on the "Roving Journeyman" family of songs (Laws H4), and in this case may have derived from the Canadian loggers' "Ye Maidens of Ontario." Note Edith F. Fowke and Richard Johnston, eds., *Folk Songs of Canada* (Waterloo, Ont.: Waterloo Music Co., 1954), pp. 76–77, and Rickaby, *Shanty-Boy*, pp. 79–81. A recorded example is the title cut for Brandon, "*Roving Irishman*," transcribed in Fowke, *Traditional Singers and Songs*, pp. 92–93.

7

Ted Ashlaw, Solitary Singer

Woods singers developed a sense of their song heritage and talent long before they took to singing in bunkhouses and barrooms. No one sat Eddie and Ted Ashlaw down as children and patiently instructed them in the nuances of carrying a tune. No one trained them in vocal projection. No one badgered them into taking formal music lessons when they'd rather be doing something else. They sought out the material. They learned how to sing by listening and imitating, building upon musical giftedness in an environment that encouraged its fruition. In short, they became "singers" by accretion, a process epitomized in the person of Ted Ashlaw. He lives at the outskirts of Hermon.

Ted Ashlaw began his logging career at the age of fifteen, when he joined Eddie to find work at North Lake and Saranac Lake. By the Beaver River job of 1923 he was an accomplished log-loader, especially admired for his deft use of a canthook (a lumberman's tool for rolling logs). With the exception of brief construction labor during the Depression, Ted spent the next twenty-four years working on various lumbering operations in the vicinity of Tupper Lake. From 1937 to 1947 he "drove tractor" and "drawed pulp" by truck on jobs managed by his brother. While the work was steady after the mid-1930s, Ted never achieved anywhere near Eddie's financial security during the World War II upsurge. Indeed, by 1947, Ted Ashlaw had experienced more than his share of personal hardship.

In 1925 Ted married a woman whom he describes as "wonderful and beautiful." She died unexpectedly from tuberculosis in 1934. "It was right in the Depression," he recalls. "I had about a thousand dollars when she got that way—when she died I didn't have anything. Had three kids and I couldn't earn enough to pay their board. I worked a whole week and got twelve dollars—if you got a rainy day, only had ten dollars. Well, pretty quick everything was gone and I was broke. Then I married again. The kids were here and there, and I wanted to make a home for them. And that marriage didn't work out, so it ended up. Then I married Helen."

Ted had begun to court Helen in 1945. He was forty at the time; she was sixteen. Ted foresaw the potential shortcomings if the relationship continued, but they were deeply in love and proceeded with the vows. That year, 1947, promised future happiness. Tragedy struck with cruel suddenness in early July. Ted was on a lumbering job for the Draper Corporation.

> There was a log hung up in a tree where we were working. Couldn't quite reach it. And some of the boys said, "Take a chain to reach it."
>
> "Nah," the foreman said, "I'll move the loader over."
>
> It was a big mistake. He moved that mechanical log-loader back across the road. And just as I went to pick up them tongs [connected to the loader], he put that boom right in the 4800-volt power line. I got electrocuted—I went straight out, rigid. Apparently (according to them) there were probably three or four minutes that I lay across them before they could get 'em out. So they went over to the truck to call in the coroner, or the doctor, or whatever they wanted. That was between 11:30 A.M. and noon. They brought me out of it at 4:00 P.M.
>
> They took me to the hospital. Had some doctors there, and electricians.
>
> And they said, "Let's slit them pants. I think he's got a bad leg."
>
> Hell, there were just little specks of burn in the pants. I dropped my pants and there was a hole 4½″ by 5″ through my right thigh. And the cords lay right in there. Current went right around them.
>
> Apparently there was an old galvanized pail that had been there in the ground. And I guess that was about where I laid. Put the clinkers to me once and for all. To this day no electricians and no doctors can understand how I ever pulled out of that one. After all, 4800 is a lot! A good many times I've wished they never went to get the fella who helped. I think I'd have been a lot better off if they'd have left me right there. Living like this is no good.

The accident left Ted partially paralyzed for two years. "Along about the fall of 1949," he told me, "I began to get feelings back. And when they came back I had too many of them." He entered a hospital in 1950 and had five discs removed from his twisted vertebrae. The recuperation was long and tedious, with many days spent immobile in a chair. It was a torturous fate for a woodsman who had spent his life in outdoor manual labor. As Ted put it, "A fella could look at it this way: if he likes to live that way, he was lucky. But if he don't, it was just one of those things, that's all."

Ted has never fully recovered from the mishap. He is able to walk now, but his ailing right leg and back are constant reminders of the suffering he has lived through. By the time he felt good enough to get around, he had reached the age when many men retire. There have been no regular jobs since he left the woods. He spends much of his time at home, playing solitaire and watching television. Legal entanglements have kept compensation benefits to a minimum. Ted has been fortunate to have loving and supportive offspring and relatives, several of whom live nearby. It has taken a strong family to weather the setbacks and recurrent periods of emotional depression, especially after Ted and Helen parted in 1972 and another marital arrangement fell through a year later. One must know these things, however tragic and unsettling, to understand the man and artist.

There is no way of determining now how many folk ballads and songs Ted actually had in his repertory earlier in life. He says that he began to learn them in his household, and from neighboring friends and woodsmen, as early as age seven. He and a boyhood companion decided to acquire as many different pieces as possible. As soon as they had learned a song they wrote its title down on a sheet of paper. By the end of World War I the inventory had grown to "way over two hundred titles." New items were picked up and performed in both domestic and occupational contexts throughout his logging days. Some songs were forgotten through time and disuse. Others made less impression and slipped from his memory as new acquisitions superseded them. So it is difficult to either verify or qualify Ted's statement that "altogether I'd knowed probably three thousand songs—get 'em from here and there and all over." Whatever the number, it was enough to single him out among peers. "There was a time," he says, "I did a *lot* of singing, and a bunch of 'em figured I was pretty good at it."

I once asked Ted how his singing reputation measured up to Eddie's. "There was a few songs Eddie used to get," he replied, "and he got them *goddamn good*, too! But he wasn't too much to go ahead and sing." Together in a barroom, it was Ted who was usually first called upon to perform. Ted claims he could "sing all night and never sing the same song twice." The remark is formulaic among distinguished woods singers but

Ted Ashlaw at home, singing "The Jam on Gerry's Rock." Hermon, N.Y., December, 1970.

nonetheless consistent with the evidence of sixty-eight ballads and songs in his repertory, at age seventy (items Ted knows but which I did not tape record are preceded by an asterisk):

"Allen Bayne," "At a Kind Old Mother's Side," "The Bad Girl's Lament," "The Banks of Little Eau Pleine," "Barbara Allen," "The Basket of Eggs," "Beaver River," "The Blind Child," "Cole Younger," "Cottage by the Sea," "Cousin Nellie," "Donny Dims of the Arrow," "Don't Send My Boy to Prison," "Down by the Sea Shore," "Driving Saw-Logs on the Plover," * "The Dying Soldier," "The Farmer's Curst Wife," "Fifteen Years Ago Today," * "The Gay Spanish Maid," * "The Goddamn Wheel," "The Gentle Boy," "Good Old Dollar Bill," "Good-bye, Jenny Jones," "Gospel of Treasure," "A Hobo's Life," "I Had a Little Girl," "I Know What It Means to Be Lonely," "The Indian Maid (Lasca)," "The Irish Mail Robber," "Jack and the Chambermaid," "Jack and Joe," "The Jam on Gerry's Rock," "Jimmy's Mother Went to See Her Son," "Joe Bowers," "Just before the Last Great Fight," "Katie Morey," "Kisses Don't Lie," "The Little Mohea," "The Little Rosewood Casket," "Mantle So Green," "Mickey Brannigan's Pup," "Miner Hill," "Message from over the Sea," "Moonlight and Skies," "Mother Was a Lady (or, If Jack Were Only Here)," "My Little Rambling Rose," "My Mother-in-Law Was Sick One Day," * "Oh No, My Boy, Not I," "Paddy Magrue," "Peggy Gordon," "A Picture from Life's Other Side," "Poor Little Joe," * "The Red-Light Saloon," "The

Rich Merchant," "'Root Hog or Die' Is Hitler's Battle Cry," "The Roving Cunningham," "Satisfied Mind," * "The Stowaway Boy," "Sunbeam in the Sky," * "The Tenderfoot," "The Trail to Mexico," "'Twas Only an Irishman's Dream," "Two Sons of North Britain," "When the Work's All Done This Fall," * "The Wild Colonial Boy," * "The Wild Mustard River," "Willie Was as Fine a Sailor," "The Young Irish Boy."

As close neighbors, Ted and Wilfred Monica learned songs from one another in youth. Very likely they sang in the same straightforward, full-throated vocal style that Ted used late in life. Both men credit Hopkinton woods singer Johnny Pelow as being their primary source of inspiration. In light of the material learned from him, Pelow was an important link in the diffusion of Anglo-Scots-Irish folksong tradition from the Canadian Maritimes, New Brunswick, and Ottawa Valley into the western Adirondack foothills. "Willie Was as Fine a Sailor" is a prime example of the type of British traditional ballad that Ted and Wilfred "picked up" from Pelow. Ted says he learned it when he was about eight or nine years old.

WILLIE WAS AS FINE A SAILOR

"O yes, I'm going to leave you, love, to plow the deep blue sea, When for-eign fac-es on me smile, it will make you dear-er to me, And if I should break my pro-mis-es, on for-eign land or here, And if you should die, I pray your ghost would haunt me ev-ery-where.

Willie was as fine a sailor as ever spliced a rope,
And Mary was his own true love, his own fond love at home.
They dearly loved each other and were to join their wedlock band,
When Willie got his orders to sail to some foreign land.

On the day that Willie was to sail, he met Mary on the strand.
"It's adieu unto you, Mary dear, for now we're doomed to part,
And I pray to God before I leave you'll pledge your aching heart."

"Oh, yes, you're going to leave me, love, to plow the deep blue sea;
When foreign faces on you smile, you'll never think of me."
For time had past true-lover's hope, and under a death's-knell sky,
"And if you should prove false to me, Willie, 'twould break my heart and I'd
    die."

"Oh yes, I'm going to leave you, love, to plow the deep blue sea;
When foreign faces on me smile, it will make you dearer to me;
And if I should break my promises, on foreign land or here,
And if you should die, I pray your ghost would haunt me everywhere."

He took one brace, in fond embrace, and then he went away.
"Aloft, aloft," the captain cried, to get our ships off to sea,
With a heavy load, twixt sea and gale, we entered into the storm.
We waltzed and danced with joy and glee, and each man drank a lot,
Till another fair damsel Willie beguiled, and Mary was forgot.

It's now our ship has cast its anchor, and once more leaves the shore,
And when it gets into deep water, we'll see the land no more,
And when it got into deep water, and under a death's-knell sky,
A dark cloud came up in the West, and a storm it did draw nigh.
And when the storm it did draw nigh, it caused our ship to reel,
And Willie, being a first-class sailor, was sent to guide the wheel.

Amidst a flash of lightning, a figure stood in his eye,
All clad in white, and when it spoke, it was like a graveyard's cry.
Saying, "Willie, Willie, you false young man, I'm Mary's ghost," said she,
"I'm here to remind you of those promises on shore you made to me."

She clasped him with her clay-cold hands, says, "Willie, come with your
    bride";
When a mountain of waves swept over them, and it washed them down the
    side.

"They're gone, they're gone," the captain cried, which shocked those men
   with fear,
When their bodies sank beneath the wave, and the night drew calm and
   clear.

Johnny Pelow was also responsible for exposing Ted to "The Braes of
Yarrow," a tragic Scots ballad of love and grief, involving the preservation of a clan's aristocratic bloodlines. Ted's title is an oral mutation of
the Scottish "dowie dens" (i.e., "dreary vale") setting in the Yarrow
River valley.

DONNY DIMS OF THE ARROW

There lived a lady in the North,
She could scarcely find her arrow;
She was courted by nine noblemen
At the donny dims of the Arrow.

These nine young men were drinking wine,
As they'd ofttimes done before;
They raised an attempt among the nine
To fight for her at the Arrow.

Her father had a young ploughboy,
And Sarah loved him dearly;

They dressed him up like a nobleman
To fight for her at the Arrow.

"Oh, will you take the hunting hounds,
Or will you take the arrow,
Or will you take the native sword
To fight for her at the Arrow?"

"I will not take the hunting hounds,
Or I will not take the arrow;
But I will take the native sword
And I'll fight for her at the Arrow."

Oh, he went way up on the high, high hill,
And down the lane so narrow;
'Twas there he spied nine noblemen
At the donny dims of the Arrow.

It's three he drew, and three he sling,
And three were badly wounded;
When her brother John from behind the bush
He shot him with his arrow.

"Go home, go home, you false young man,
And tell your sister Sarah
That her true-love John is dead and gone
At the donny dims of the Arrow."

"Oh, mother dear, I had a dream,
I hope it proves no sorrow;
I dreamed my true-love John was dead
At the donny dims of the Arrow."

"Oh, daughter dear, dry up your tears,
And weep no more for sorrow;
For a fairer a rose never bloomed in June
Than the one you've lost at the Arrow."

She went way up on the high, high hill,
And down the lane so narrow,
And there she spied her true-love John,
He was dead and gone at the Arrow.

She washed his face and combed his hair,
As she'd ofttimes done before;

She wrapped a cloth around his slate
And drew him to her arrow.

"Now, mother dear, you have seven sons,
You may wed them all tomorrow;
But as fair a rose never bloomed in June
As the one I lost at the Arrow."

Johnny Pelow's influence upon Ted in childhood domestic surroundings laid the groundwork for swapping and learning songs in the woods.
The carryover was inevitable for a boy born in a lumbercamp, a boy who
seasonally saw the likes of Johnny Pelow shift from tossing hay to rolling
logs. Ted was about twelve years old when he met "a comical old Irish
fella from Vermont" named Pete Celoon. One of Celoon's songs was an
Irish-American comic ditty entitled "Mickey Brannigan's Pup." It wasn't
long before Ted was singing it himself:

MICKEY BRANNIGAN'S PUP

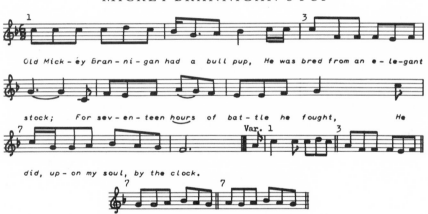

Old Mickey Brannigan had a bull pup,
He was bred from an elegant stock;
For seventeen hours of battle he fought,
He did, upon my soul, by the clock.

His tail was a neat little bit of a stub;
Bowlegged with two crooked eyes.
By the look of his snaggle-tooth's mug was enough
For the devil himself in disguise.

Bow-wow-wow, what a dog to be sure,
When at fighting he'd never give up.
There never was no such a wonderful dog
As old Mickey Brannigan's pup.

For he tore the tail off from Maloney's best coat,
The bustle of Mary Ann Flynn,
And he ran between young Kitty Mulligan's legs—
Now truly weren't that a sin!

He cut up the little Dutch shoemaker's dog,
He shook him around like a rat;
He murdered Tom Owens' most wonderful goat
And the tail of McManus' cat!

Bow-wow-wow, what a dog to be sure,
When at fighting he'd never give up.
There never was no such a wonderful dog
As old Mickey Brannigan's pup.

There's a man he came 'round with an organ one day
And a monkey tied fast by a string.
And when the pup saw him he held with delight
And he made a most wonderful spring!

He grabbed for the organ grinder and all,
He murdered the organ inside.
And b'heavens he tried for to swallow the monk
And he choked on his tail and he *died!*

And so Ted Ashlaw's song repertory grew through his repeated exposure to other woods singers in area homes, remote bunkhouses, and public barrooms. Learning new material from itinerant performers like Charlie Cunningham became an enjoyable challenge. Recalls Ted,

There's some songs, where I thought some of 'em was kind of sketchy, I'd just jot down a little bit of it, something like that, if I knew he was going to be gone. And then, if I didn't get them, the next time I saw him in camp I'd get him to sing that one, the one I wanted. Jesus, we'd have him sing 'em over—anything we thought we liked. We'd have him sing it over again and again.

Once in a while there'd be somebody who'd get pretty drunk, and he couldn't sing at all, and try it. Hell, you wasn't going to say nothing. He was just happy, he was trying to do it. If they were feeling good maybe they thought they were singing. But it sounded like they should have put a horse collar on them or something. I'd pay no attention to him.

There is a mysterious and wonderful bond that can develop, over time, between a fieldworker and field contact. I suspect it is born from respect and appreciation, and nurtured by the chemistry of discovery. With Ted Ashlaw, I sensed that process from the first cups of instant coffee we consumed together two days after Christmas, in 1970; with Ham and Eddie, the sociable beers meant much the same. Talks with Ted brought me close to a folk artist devoid of pretension, a traditional singer who downplayed the larger importance of his folk artistry and repertory surviving in an age of young urban-based folksong interpreters.

Early in our talks, I discovered that Ted knew nothing of the several hundred record companies that in recent years have pressed countless field recordings and reissues of early commercial recordings. True, he owns several well-worn anthology albums featuring the Carter Family from the 1930s—a cherished reminder of times past. He found the LPs in the discount stack of a local food store, interspersed with modern country-western releases. But he couldn't imagine that much else in that vein was available, what with the usual music heard on his radio. Ted observed in 1972 after singing "Barbara Allen," for instance, that he had never heard it on a record, nor had he seen it in print. For him it was but another of the "good ones" learned many years earlier from oral tradition—"good ones" that sometimes included surprises, such as his "Paddy Magrue," an unexpurgated version of "Little Musgrave and Lady Barnard," another seventeenth-century Scottish ballad.

PADDY MAGRUE

The first came in was a scar-let pink, The next was the sky-lit blue, And the next came in was Lord Van-a-bill's wife, The fair-est one of the two.

Var. 1-2

The first came in was a scarlet pink,
The next was a sky-lit blue,
And the next came in was Lord Vanabill's wife,
The fairest one of the two.

"It's home with me, now Paddy Magrue,
It's home with me, I say.
And oh, what a time and a time and a time,
And oh, what a time we'll have."

"Oh no, oh no," cried Pat,
"Oh no, not for my life.
I can tell by the ring that's on your finger
You are Lord Vanabill's wife."

"Suppose'n I am Lord Vanabill's wife?
Lord Vanabill isn't at home.
He has gone to King Kennen's castle
And tonight I must sleep alone."

A man overheard the conversation,
He jumped right up and he ran,
He ran till he came to the riverside,
He jumped right in and he swam.

He swam till he came to the other side,
He jumped right up and he ran,
He ran till he came to King Kennen's castle,
He rapped so hard that it rang.

"Who come there, my boy?" said he,
"Oh, who come there, I say?
Is any my castle walls torn down,
Or any my victories won?"

"There's none of your castle walls torn down,
Or none of your victories won;
But Paddy Magrue is in bed with your wife,
The likes that ain't ever yet known."

"Now, if it's a lie you're telling to me,
Which I suppose it will be,
I'll build a scaffold in fair Scotland
And hanged man you will be."

"Oh, if it's a lie I'm telling to you,
Which you suppose it will be,
Don't build no scaffold in fair Scotland,
But hang me up to a tree."

Now, they conversed for around an hour or two,
And they both fell asleep.
They never awoke till the very next morning;
Lord Vanabill stood at their feet.

"Now, how do you like my bed?" said he,
"And how do you like my sheets?
And how do you like that pretty fair maid
That lies in your arms asleep?"

"Oh, well I like your bed," said Pat,
"And well I like your sheets.
And better I like that pretty fair maid
That lies in my arms asleep."

"Get up and dress yourself," said he,
"Get up and dress, I say.
I wouldn't have it said in fair Scotland
For killing an undressed man."

"Oh no, oh no," cried Pat,
"Oh no, not for my life,
For on your side you have two swords,
And I've not even a knife."

"If on my side I have two swords,
I paid for them deep in my purse.
You may take the very best one
And I will take the worst.

"And you may strike the very first blow;
Strike it like a man.
And I will strike the very next blow
And kill you if I can."

Magrue he struck the very first blow;
He wounded Lord Vanabill sore.
Lord Vanabill struck the very next blow
And Magrue couldn't screw any more.

I think Ted was mildly amused whenever I became excited about some of the seldom-recorded pieces in his repertory (e.g., "Willie Was as Fine a Sailor"), and I quickly learned the limits and dangers of preconceptions. Ted has been unencumbered by the academic distinctions of song type and the puzzles of song origin and geographical distribution through time that keep folksong scholars busy, and the term "folksong," for instance, remains alien both to his vocabulary and to his way of grouping songs.

Still, one would expect a singer like Ted Ashlaw to have some system for distinguishing one group of songs from another. In view of the foothills heritage, labels like "river-drive songs" or "dirty songs" might be predictable, and Ted does respond to them in conversation. The greater surprise, during discussions spanning seven years, was the infrequency with which he spontaneously introduced those terms. He spoke instead of his "songs," calling all of them "good ones," and dividing them basically into "old, old songs" picked up between 1912 and 1923, and "old songs" learned during the period 1924–47. For him, the meaningful categories lay along a time continuum, roughly the logging years preceding and those following the Beaver River operation. Prior to the mid-1920s, fellow woods singers Johnny Pelow, Wilfred Monica, and Charlie Cunningham were his prime sources for learning new material; thereafter, increasing exposure to local barroom singers, 78 rpm records, and Nashville-influenced radio programs filled out his repertory.

Ted's concept of "old, old songs," in other words, has no necessary correlation with the actual age of a given piece. He has no reservations whatsoever in setting eighteenth-century British ballads (e.g., "Gospel of Treasure") alongside late Victorian and Tin Pan Alley lyrics (e.g., "A Picture from Life's Other Side"). Nor, in the case of his "old songs," is he the least unsettled to hear that items like "Just before the Last Great Fight," from the 1860s and originally entitled "The Battle of Fredericksburg," is historically more than seventy-five years older than his version of Ernest Tubb's lyric "I Know What It Means to Be Lonely" (Decca 6064, 1941).

For a long time I thought that Ted's ordering of his songs went no further. But reviewing my tapes in August, 1972, I began to notice that he also earmarked individual songs by textual length. Unobtrusively, perhaps even unconsciously, he had revealed what perhaps is the segmented framework of his personal repertory. I hasten here to emphasize the uncertainty factor: when I later presented Ted with my taxonomy, he remarked only that he had "never thought about it like that before."

Among the "old, old songs," Ted calls ballads with ten or more stanzas "big, long ones." That includes the four anonymous folk ballads of English and Scottish pedigree, and a cross-section of the British broadside and native American ballads. "Two Sons of North Britain" and "Cole Younger" illustrate the latter variety. The first of these songs appears in a Scottish songster dated 1778 and bears the stamp of Scottish Loyalist sympathies during the Revolutionary War. Ted's version required five minutes to perform.

TWO SONS OF NORTH BRITAIN

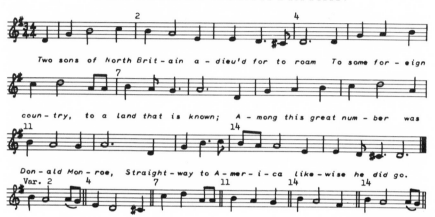

Two sons of North Britain adieu'd for to roam
To some foreign country, to a land that is known;
Among this great number was Donald Monroe,
Straightway to America likewise he did go.

He having two sons with their uncle to stay,
The price of their passage he couldn't well pay.
Saying, "Are you contented with your uncle here?
The price of your passage you know would be dear."

Now, they being discontented they rode till they found
A ship all in anchor for America bound.
Here they both enlisted, crossed over the main
In hopes for to find their dear parents again.

Now, when they had landed on America's side,
Surrounded by ruffians on every side,
With humble submission to their good captain went
To see if they might gain their good captain's consent.

To go up the country their parents to see,
Here they left their good captain,
Took a boy for their guide
To show them the place where their parents reside.

As they walked along together these two brothers did say,
"If we could but find our dear parents today,
It would much surprise them to see us once more,
For of our enlisting I'm sure they don't know."

They walked along a little farther till they came to a grove
Where the trees and the branches did all seem to move.
There being two ruffians concealed in these woods,
And they prompted their rifles where the two brothers stood.

And lodging two bullets within their two breasts,
Saying, "We'll take all their money
And take all their clothes,
And if they're yet living we'll deal them more blows."

Oh, one being a-living he raised up his head.
"You murderous villain," these words he then said.
"You murderous villain, you bloodthirsty hounds,
Oh, why did you murder us before we had found,

"Before we had found our dear parents again.
We left them in Scotland seven, twelve months ago;
Perhaps you might know them—
Their names are Monroe."

"You being my son, then," the old man replied,
"Who is the young fellow that lies by your side?"
"He is my only brother and your youngest son;
Do you blame your heart ever for the deed you have done?

"Now, if you're my father," the boy then replied,
"I'm glad that I saw you before that I died.
Tell not our old mother if she does yet live
That we were both murdered, for fear she might grieve."

Cole Younger rode with the band of Confederate desperadoes known as Quantrill's Raiders, later joining the notorious James brothers. Ted's ballad, "one of Cunningham's," chronicles an actual ill-fated robbery on September 7, 1876. Younger was captured soon after the incident and spent twenty-five years in the Stillwater prison. Pulp writers of the day turned him into a celebrity, and upon release he toured the country in a Wild West show.

COLE YOUNGER

I am a poor lone bandit man, and Cole Younger is my name; I've committed many a depredation that brought my folks to shame; I'm a robber of the Northfield Bank, the same I'll never deny, And it leaves me now a prisoner in Stillwater Jail to die.

I am a poor lone bandit man, and Cole Younger is my name;
I've committed many a depredation that brought my folks to shame;
I'm a robber of the Northfield Bank, the same I'll never deny,
And it leaves me now a prisoner in Stillwater Jail to die.

The first of my depredations I mean for to let you know
Was a California miner, and we robbed him of his gold.
We robbed him of his gold, my boys, and that without delay,
And on returning home that day my brother Jim did say:

"Now, Cole, we'll buy fast horses, we'll ride so far away,
We'll be avenged of our father's death, together we will stay.
We'll fight them like guerillas, Cole, until the day we die"—
And it leaves me now a prisoner in Stillwater Jail to die.

We started out for Texas, that good old Lone Star State,
'Twas along the Nebraska prairie where the James boys we did meet.

With our bright shining knives and revolvers we all sat down to play;
We had plenty of good old "tiger's blood" to pass the time away.

The Union Pacific Railroad being the next that we did surprise;
To see the work from our bloody hands would bring the tears to your eyes.
'Twas along the Nebraska prairie where the dead and wounded lie—
And it leaves me now a prisoner in Stillwater Jail to die.

We mounted to our horses and northward we did go,
To that godforsaken country called Minneso-tee-o.
Our plans were fixed on the Northfield Bank when Jesse James did say,
"Now, Cole, if you undertake that job you'll surely ruin the day."

We stationed out our pickets and straightaway to the bank did go.
I stood before the counter when I struck that dreadful blow.
"Hand over all of your money, boys, and that without delay;
We are those noted highwaymen and we give you no time to pray."

"Oh hark! What is that dreadful noise is heard above our cries?"
When Jesse James came running in, saying, "Boys, we are surprised."
For the first volley that they gave us, Bill Chadwell he went down,
And next it was my brother Jim received a deathly wound.

We mounted to our horses, my brother Jim and I,
And from his wounds along the ground the crimson gore did lie.
When Jesse James rode up to us and this to me did say,
"Now, Cole, if you don't dispose of Jim we'll never get away."

But I being a noted outlaw, I'd been through blood and strife;
I swore that I would kill the man that would take my brother's life.
It was there we parted company, the James boys and I—
And it leaves me now a prisoner in Stillwater Jail to die.

For "old, old songs" ranging from six to ten stanzas in length, Ted speaks of "long ones"; for everything shorter, "little ones." Once again, these subcategories contain a mixture of British and native American pieces learned directly from other foothills singers. Among the ballads, for example, one finds the "long one" "Joe Bowers," a California Gold Rush favorite; Ted's version runs eight stanzas. A "little one," at four stanzas, is a lament entitled "The Gentle Boy," previously collected in Newfoundland.

THE GENTLE BOY

'Twas on one dark and stormy night, as I lay me down to sleep,
I heard a boy 'bout six years old, by his mother's side did weep,
Saying, "Once I had a father who kindly of me did embrace,
And if he were here, he'd wipe those tears flow down my mother's face.

"Why don't my father's ship return, and why don't he come home?
While other ships come sailing in while spreading the ocean foam,
Why don't my father's ship return, and why don't he come home?

"He said he'd be 'bout six months gone, leaving you and I alone;
The wintry winds have blown, mama, six months have passed and gone.
And other ships they come sailing in while spreading the ocean foam,
Why don't my father's ship return, and why don't he come home?

"He said he'd bring some buds and flowers from off that far India tree;
But the wintry winds have blown, six months have passed and gone.
And these other ships they come sailing in spreading the ocean foam,
Why don't my father's ship return, and why don't he come home?"

"My Little Rambling Rose," another "little one," illustrates the striking juxtapositions of song type that occur within the taxonomy. Ted says he learned the World War I parlor song from Wilfred Monica.

MY LITTLE RAMBLING ROSE

They called her "Rambling Rose" because she used to love to stray,
They called her "Rambling Rose" because she always had her way.
She rambled to a city from a town she thought was dead;
Her sweetheart wrote a note, and this is what it read:

"Some day you'll ramble back to me, my little Rambling Rose,
You'll come back home, no more to roam; I want you, goodness knows;
You'll soon be tired of city life, of all the world and noise and strife;
Then you'll come back to be my wife, my little Rambling Rose."

But she loved the lights on Broadway, and she loved the world and strife,
She loved to dine at Rector's with a lot of college boys.
Then one day there came a longing for the one she used to miss;
She wrote a little note to him, and all it read was this:
"I'm tired of all those city joys, of all the world and noise and boys.
I'm coming back for old-time joys, your little Rambling Rose."

Ted's "long ones" and "little ones" subdivisions apply also to his "old songs" category. Absent, or at least unarticulated in interviews, is the "big long ones" designation. He seems to reserve that terminology exclusively for the lengthy ballads from the early years. It is conceivable that the songs he acquired after 1923 just happened to be shorter than ten stanzas. Perhaps, on the other hand, longer pieces simply failed to surface during our get-togethers. I have no easy explanation for the anomaly; maybe looking for one is unwarranted, too much the quest for neatness and symmetry in a domain of artistry. Among his "old long ones," Ted does single out "The Indian Maid" ("Lasca") as memorable. Its Old West subject matter suggests the repertory links with other western Adirondack singers like brother Eddie, and Ham Ferry.

LASCA

I once did love an In-dian maid, A-las-ka was her name, 'Way
out in sun-ny Tex-as, on that wild and dis-mal plain; She could
ride a fi-ery bron-co, or rope a steer as he passed by; She could

shoot   a   ri - fle   or   a   bow,   and   kill   a   bird   on   high.
Var. 1   1-2   5

5   6-7

I once did love an Indian maid, Alaska was her name,
'Way out in sunny Texas, on that wild and dismal plain;
She could ride a fiery bronco, or rope a steer as he passed by;
She could shoot a rifle or a bow, and kill a bird on high.

I made her jealous of me one day, took a damsel out to ride;
She plunged a dagger at my heart that barely missed my side.
Just one inch further to the left, I'd have failed to breathe again,
And the vultures they would have picked my bones, out on that dismal plain.

As we were riding out one morn, the weather being fine and warm,
And all at once the sky drew dark, there came up an awful storm.
The wind it soon began to blow, it blew with might and main,
The air was filled with dust and sand, and it soon began to rain.

"Hop on your horse," Alaska cried, "we'll scour the distant plain,
For perhaps we will find shelter if we ride with might and main."
We rode until our horses dropped, no shelter could we find,
And the exchange it was coming, it was coming close behind.

"Under your horse," Alaska cried, "here lies our only chance."
Ten thousand herd they were coming, ten thousand cattle advanced.
Ten thousand herd they were coming, you could hear them beller and roar,
You could feel the ground shake and tremble as they came galloping o'er.

They came and went, the storm was o'er, I sat and gazed around.
Not a blade of grass that could be seen, the plains were like plowed ground.
She had thrown her arms around my neck, my breast had pillowed her head,
And when at last my mind came back I found that she was dead.

I buried her on a shady knoll out on that distant plain,
Down by a little briary stream that flowed through rocks and sand,

And on her grave I carved a cross, and on it I carved a hand;
Plainly laid it to the space where my true-love died on the banks of the Rio Grande.

Now, I'll go back to old Texas, but her grave I will keep green,
For the waters of the Rio Grande from a distance it can been seen.
Once more I will be a cowboy, and cattle I'll herd and brand;
But her missing I'll keep secret on the banks of the Rio Grande.

Usually, Ted volunteered a couple of "little ones" to wrap up our sessions together, explaining that those songs take "less wind to sing." "There was a time there," he says, "when you could put a record on—of Carl Smith, Roy Acuff, Lefty Frizzell, or anybody—and by the time I'd learned that song and sung it, you'd think it was him. I've always been like that: I could do it just like they could, with the same voice. Most generally, one of them songs would come along, and you'd kind of forget it." One Ted hasn't forgotten is an 1896 composition, "Mother Was a Lady (or, If Jack Were Only Here)," a vaudeville hit that he "got off a record thirty years ago."

MOTHER WAS A LADY
(OR, IF JACK WERE ONLY HERE)

tear-drops to her eyes: "My moth-er was a la-dy, and yours, she would al-

low, And you may have a sis-ter who needs pro-tec-tion now; I

came to this great cit-y to find my broth-er dear,

You would-n't dare in-sult me, sir, if broth-er Jack were here."

Two drummers, they were seated in a grand hotel one day;
While dining, they were chatting in a jovial sort of way;
There came a pretty waitress to bring a tray of food,
They spoke to her familiarly in a manner rather rude.
At first she didn't notice or make the least reply,
But one remark was made to her, brought teardrops to her eyes:

> "My mother was a lady, and yours, she would allow,
> And you may have a sister who needs protection now;
> I came to this great city to find my brother dear,
> You wouldn't dare insult me, sir, if brother Jack were here."

These two sat there in silence, their heads hung in shame;
"Forgive me, miss, we meant no harm—pray tell me, what's your name?"
She told him and he cried aloud, "I know your brother, too!
We've been friends for many, many years, and he often speaks of you.
Come go with me when I go back, and if you'll only wed,
I'll take you to him as my bride, for I loved you since you said":

> Chorus:

Ted remains outspoken about his personal taste in music. Invariably, he contrasts the "goddamn inky-dinky stuff they've got today" with the kinds of materials he liked and learned in the past. "I always thought these older songs had something *to it*," he stresses.

They were more of the story right through than something over and over, and then that title coming in forty or fifty times in the three-minute record. The songs of today ain't nothing like they used to be. Used to be a song was a *song!* It weren't the two, three words sung over and over and call it a song, like they got on the records.

Twenty-five or thirty years ago, Dave Denny had his own radio station in Albany. And they were wanting for songs. All he'd holler: "Get the title in the song! Get the title in the songs!" Unless that title was in there ten or fifteen times, he wouldn't accept it. Well, jeepers, when you get all done, that's all you had, was the title. Well, what the hell was the good of just the title? Any goddamn fool can say something in two or three little verses, and then say it again, and keep saying it all through. I don't call them "songs."

All this popular stuff, that there's just a bitter pill for me. I just can't go it! 'Course, there's other people that have their own ideas, I suppose. I can see their point there, too, where mostly now what they're after is something to *dance* on—so it doesn't matter if they say anything at all. But I couldn't see that being a "song."

As Ted observes, it's the aesthetics of much contemporary popular music that he objects to, rather than the mass media per se. His repertory confirms that point. In 1925 or 1926, for example, his father-in-law purchased a Victor phonograph from woods singer Elmer Jones. Included in the deal were several 78 rpm records featuring early hillbilly artists singing traditional folksongs, "Driving Saw-Logs on the Plover" among them, which Ted set about learning.

DRIVING SAW-LOGS ON THE PLOVER

saw-logs on the Plov-er, and you'll nev-er get your pay.

There were some shady Plover banks one evening last July,
A mother of a shantyboy, and doleful was her cry,
Saying, "God be with you, Johnny, although you're far away,
Driving saw-logs on the Plover, and you'll never get your pay.

"Oh Johnny, you were your father's hope, your mother's only joy;
Why is it that you ramble so, my own, my darling boy?
And why induce you, Johnny, from your own dear home to stray,
Driving saw-logs on the Plover, and you'll never get your pay?

"You had better stay upon the farm, and feed the ducks and hens,
And drive the pigs and sheep each night, and put them in their pens;
Be better for you to help your dad to cut his corn and hay,
Than to drive saw-logs on the Plover, and you'll never get your pay."

A log canoe came floating as down the quiet stream,
As peacefully it glided as some young lover's dream.
A youth crept out upon the bank, and this to her did say,
"Oh, mother dear, I have quit the game, and I haven't got my pay.

"The boys call me a 'sucker' and a 'son-of-a-gun' to boot;
I said to myself, 'Now, Johnny, it's time for you to scoot.'
I stole a canoe and started upon my dreary way,
And now I'm back home again, and never a cent of pay."

Now, all young men, take this advice if you ever wish to roam,
Be sure and kiss your mother before you leave your home.
But you'd better stay upon the farm for a half-a-dollar a day,
Then to drive saw-logs on the Plover, and you'll never get your pay.

Above all else, Ted values accurate representation of material. The majority of Northeast traditional singers share that aesthetic ideal, though

they customarily introduce subtle vocal and melodic variations into successive renditions of a given song. Ted certainly does. In his case, the nuances seem largely unconscious, or at least unselfconscious. He says that he never tried to achieve a distinctive, idiosyncratic "sound." In practice that occasionally meant adhering to garbled words, to the declamando endings learned along with pieces like "The Jam on Gerry's Rock" and "Mickey Brannigan's Pup," or to other mannerisms. The personal pleasure of knowing songs and being able to sing them "right" motivated him from the beginning. His striving to duplicate a respected singer was a statement of admiration, a tribute to someone drawn closer by the very act of close imitation.

Not surprisingly, Ted assumes that his version of a folksong is the correct one. During the summer of 1972, for instance, when he heard a recorded interpretation of "The Wild Colonial Boy" broadcast over a Canadian radio station, his response said a lot about his aesthetic and his pride as a folk artist: "I knowed that before he ever did—he ain't even singing it right!"

That comment, together with the attitudes that prompted it, suggests some of the links between the Ashlaw brothers as woods singers. There is much that unites them: the family and friendship ties, the work and singing experiences, the feisty artistic temperaments. And, like Eddie, Ted has tried his hand at songmaking, inspired by the example of Johnny Pelow's "Miner Hill." Pelow, says Ted, "wrote out" that rollicking lumbercamp song sometime between 1915 and 1917, its subject matter the Lake Ozonia crew Ted knew as a boy. "Of course, I was awful young. But now and then, I guess I had my nose stuck in—he'd be saying something, and now and then I'd stick in a word."

MINER HILL

Come boys, if you'll lis-ten, I'll sing you a song, If you'll pay at-ten-tion, it won't take me long; It's up here at Cut-ting's, at Camp Num-ber One, The boys call the firm there Cut-ting And Son, Der-ry

down,   down, dey der - ry down.

Come boys, if you'll listen, I'll sing you a song.
If you'll pay attention, it won't take me long;
It's up here at Cutting's, at Camp Number One,
The boys call the firm there Cutting and Son,
    Derry down, down, dey derry down.

Now, the camp it is run by a Fort Jackson pet;
You all know him well, it's Levi Fayette,
    Refrain:

Miss Fayette is our cook, she is big and fat,
She's got lots to do but she doesn't mind that.
She's got lots to do, so I've heard her tell;
But she gets right around and she does it up well,
    Refrain:

Now, two in the morning the foreman would call
To wake up the teamsters, likewise Mike, his son,
Saying, "Come on there, you teamsters, and get out of that,
Go and feed those big horses and throw on the straps,"
    Refrain:

There's but nine loaders, there's three in each gang;
We loaded our loads and the binders we sprang.
We loaded our loads with both strength and skill,
For they're all damn poor skidways up around Miner Hill,
    Refrain:

Now, there's Myron Planty, he drives the big blacks,
He's on the lead and he hurries right back.
He drives to the skidway four times every day,
And said, "Roll them on, boys, and I'll haul them away,"
    Refrain:

Arthur Binan, he drives the big bays,
He's always happy while hooked to the sleighs.

He works his team both early and late;
No other team there their eveners dare take,
   Refrain:

But his brother, Lawrence, can't do quite so well,
For his old team is all shot to hell,
   Refrain:

His little nigh mare she's not very fat,
And he said, "I don't care, by the bald-headed cat!"
   Refrain:

There's but one more teamster, big George Supernault;
He ought to be dealt with according to law.
For he whips them poor horses, it's surely a sin;
He's got a long whip with a·chain on the end,
   Refrain:

Now, whiskey and poker they do not allow:
One is a nuisance, the other violates the law.
So we'd say to the blacksmith, "Let's have a few pots."
He said, "Go get the boys and we'll play in the shop,"
   Refrain:

Now our logs are all landed down on the railroad,
When our checks are made out we'll go down the tote road,
   Refrain:

Now, some will buy a quart, and perhaps three or four;
But be damned if they'd work for Fayette anymore,
   Refrain:

Ted was ready to compose his own woods song by the time he reached
Beaver River. With "Miner Hill" as the model, he set to work. "I had
them all in there, all the fellas you liked: Eddie was in it, Howard Haines,
and Smith, and John Davignon—all the lumbermen were stuck in there
some way." The end product, "Beaver River," took "one to two weeks"
to complete. "Some little thing would come up and I'd chalk it down.
And then the trouble was to get it together from one chunk I wrote to the
other. Sometimes I'd have to think of something to put in, between there,
to make it come out." When I recorded the piece in 1971, Ted said that it
was his first opportunity to sing it in thirty years. He couldn't "get together" the concluding stanza or two.

"Now our logs are all landed down on the railroad. . . ." The line from "Miner Hill" also fits this scene at Brandreth, N.Y., where the Ashlaw brothers once worked. Photograph courtesy of Edward Ashlaw.

BEAVER RIVER

Come boys, if you'll lis-ten, I'll sing you a song, If you'll

pay good at-ten-tion, it won't take me long; It's up at Bea-ver Riv-er, a

place you know well, And it's not far from Tup-per, but clos-er to

Hell, Der-ry down, down, dey der-ry down.

Come boys, if you'll listen, I'll sing you a song,
If you'll pay good attention, it won't take me long;
It's up at Beaver River, a place you know well,
And it's not far from Tupper, but closer to Hell,
   Derry down, down, dey derry down.

When I first came to Beaver I got in there late,
Quit a good job at Saranac, came there for a stake.
The first job I landed was for my brother, Ed;
He had a pulp job from his chum old Hedge,
   Refrain:

The very next morning our troubles began:
To find us a camp or a shack to stay in.
When Paradise to Eddie said, "A camp I can get."
He says, "If you can, why, you'll go and get it,"
   Refrain:

Paradise he started, he wasn't gone long,
Came back with a story twice long as my song.
For that Paradise he lied, it is surely a sin;
He'll talk for two hours and not say a thing,
   Refrain:

But he got the camp, and that I will say;
But he told us right then we couldn't move in that day,
   Refrain:

For his brother-in-law, Haines, he had figured on that, too;
But he's full of big plans that he never can do,
   Refrain:

Smith was the first man had this job, you know;
But 'course he was under this big John Davignon.
But Harry Smith, he wasn't there long
When to John Davignon someone else sucked around,
   Refrain:

The next man had this job it was Howard Haines;
And he's just as big a man but I believe less brains,
   Refrain:

One day, says Eddie, he needed some pants,
Says as he went to dinner he went by Haines' camp.

"The very next morning our troubles began: To find us a camp or a shack to stay in . . ." (from "Beaver River"). Photograph courtesy of the Adirondack Museum.

> As he was a-walking around that way
> A man would be surprised to hear what he heard Haines say,
>   Refrain:
>
> Haines was inquiring about the Canadian job
> As he walked to the swamp with his two little "Frogs,"
>   Refrain:
>
> Now, it's over at Smitty's, where the gamblers do dwell,
> Till one night two Polacks came in to raise hell.
> Smith grabbed for his club, he got hit in his hand,
> And he made for the Polack and called his hard man,
>   Refrain:

Asked about "Beaver River," Ted will stress that the song is faithful to the way "things actually happened." Pressed on that matter, however, he confesses to exercising some artistic liberties in setting down the "truth." Take stanza 7: "I think the 'truth' of it was that old Kelly was the one who fired Smith and turned that job over to Howard Haines. But that didn't rhyme good, so I put it the other way." What about the unflattering portrayal of Paradise, three stanzas earlier? "Where you get a lot of that stuff is something you hear. Now like Paradise: that all came about by hearing. He was blabbing about something one day and somebody said to him, 'You goddamn liar, you talk all day and don't say nothing!' Well, that's where I got that. He wasn't that way, really—he just laughed about it. Paradise was right there when I wrote it!" And as for the scathing report on Howard Haines: "He was a good lumberman. He knew his business, and he was a good guy to work for. Howard Haines, I'd say, was the best man I ever worked for." So what might pass for criticism, to "some stranger," was a sham. When composed in 1923, "Beaver River" was another example of playful assault on fellow loggers in positions of occupational stature. Songmakers Ted and Eddie Ashlaw have long shared that sense of humor.

The comparisons between Ted and Eddie could go on. Ted, for instance, admits to being more introspective than his older brother, and more reticent among strangers. "I never was no hand to mix," he says. In my experience, moreover, Ted never exhibited his brother's degree of repertory possessiveness. If anything, his disposition was just the opposite. Eddie, who knows he can sing, likes to exercise his options. For reasons discussed, he often declines to perform. Ted, on the other hand, has been beset since 1972 by chronic chest ailments. Resigned to a variety of health problems and loss of wind, he deeply regrets that he is no longer able to exercise those options. For him it is a situation of cruel misfortune, for by choice he would sing frequently. In his most reflective moments, he would like nothing better than to step back in time, to before his woods accident, when he believes he could have pursued his talent to possibly become a commercially successful country entertainer.

It is for this reason, surely, that Ted so often spoke of Charlie Cunningham. Ted remembers Charlie as a "little bum" from Saranac Lake. "He had no education at all. He got drunk and froze to death in a barn. Young man, too. Hell, he wasn't probably thirty-two or thirty-three years old." Ted was nineteen then, hardworking and impressionable. He had met Charlie on the Beaver River operation. Both men were singers who had come into their own. But in Ted's eyes, Charlie Cunningham was someone special.

> He was a guy who'd come into camp and get a job as a choreboy. That's all he ever did. And you might get a song or two while he was there. But that sonofabitch wasn't a guy to stay. If he stayed a week, that was a long time for him.
>
> Sometimes you could get him to sing, and other times he was just as pigheaded as he could be. About the only time you *could* get him to sing all night

was if he was drinking—somebody'd buy him a drink or something. He was *tops*, a *good* singer! And the best part of it was that he'd make it up as he'd go and sing it to you. Just mention something and he'd go and sing a song about it. He'd have been a millionaire, and he died a drunk.

We had a camp over at Beaver River, and he come over there. He was there a couple of days. 'Course, we was working and he was drunk. You'd tell him what you wanted the song about, and he could just go ahead and do it. And that was his song from then on: he could sing it any time he wanted, just the way he done it the first. Why, I never saw anybody like him!

If there was any drinks in it, he'd sing. He'd sit in one of them barrooms and wait for somebody to buy him a drink. And he'd bum this one and bum that one.

He was sitting in a barroom in Tupper Lake one time, in the corner with this guy Jardine. Said his brother had a farm (his brother didn't have nothing more than he did), he was telling about his brother's farm.

"Of course," he said, "cow has four tits, and generally my brother lets the calves go with the cow. A lot of times they had four calves. Each one had a tit. But one of the cows had five calves. It made it bad."

"Yeah," Jardine said. "It would make it bad. What the hell would the fifth calf do?"

He said, "He'd sit back and look on, same as I'm doing."

And somebody said, "You sonofabitch! Come up here and get a drink!"

For all his admiration, Ted is nonetheless unrelenting in portraying Charlie as a marvel who ultimately wasted his talent, a man who "had just as well been into money, and he was nothing but a drunken bum." It is impossible now to ask Charlie Cunningham about his skill at "bumming" drinks through song and story. And was he really as spontaneously creative as Ted has always believed? Ted long ago answered those questions to his own satisfaction. Thus, in one sense it matters little that Cunningham's "A Hobo's Life," a song that Ted credits to Charlie's creative genius, happens to be a personalized recomposition of an eighteenth-century traditional English drinking song collected in Ontario under the title "The Faggot Cutter." For as sung by Charlie in a barroom, and learned by Ted in a lumbercamp, "A Hobo's Life" came across as original and autobiographical:

A HOBO'S LIFE

I'll tell you 'bout some rich young man that stays to home with

ease,   And he'll go   to work   at sev-en o'-clock,   and

quit when-ev-er he please; He gets his pa-pers and reads   them, and

throws them on the ground, He drinks his wine, he has good time — drink

REFRAIN:

round, my boys, drink round.   Drink round, my boys,   drink

round a-gain, un-til it comes to me,   For the long-er we sit

Var. 7

here and drink, sure the hap-pi-er we will be.

My secrets now I will unfold to all young men that's here:
Young women are good company, but I would wed with none,
And if all mankind were of my mind, young women would live alone.

I'll tell you 'bout some rich young man that stays to home with ease,
And he'll go to work at seven o'clock, and quit whenever he please;
He gets his papers and reads them, and throws them on the ground,
He drinks his wine, he has good time—drink round, my boys, drink round.

   Drink round, my boys, drink round again, until it comes to me,
   For the longer we sit here and drink, sure the happier we will be.

For a hobo's life is a pleasant one, I'll tell you the reason why:
Both day and night he sleeps with delight, he hears no baby's cry.
He may not sleep in a feather bed, but it's just the same on the ground,
For as long as he's got a quart of Old Hi's—drink round, my boys, drink
   round.

   Drink round, my boys, drink round again, until it comes to me,
   For the longer we sit here and drink, the happier we will be.

Now, he owes no debts, he has no frets, and troubles he has none,
And no man in life can kiss his wife when he is far from home.

Charlie, in Ted's eyes, represents a tragedy of intemperance, an unforgettable bunkhouse singer and barroom bard who was unable to rec-
oncile drink, song, and socializing in an appropriate way. In itself, the
singing-drinking mix was very much in keeping with woods singing.
Often, in contexts where alcohol was available, recognized woods singers
provided entertainment while appreciative companions provided verbal
and liquid stimuli. "They couldn't get me going until I was half lit," notes
Ted. I have singled out that reciprocity and its implications among western Adirondack woodsmen, but the pattern is by no means unique to the
foothills heritage. Indeed, were it less normative, men like Ted might be
much more charitable in their estimations of a singer like Charlie. For
Charlie overstepped the boundaries of acceptable propriety, satisfying
personal need at the expense of durable respect among peers.

In Eddie Ashlaw's hands, adaptation of "The Roving Journeyman" ce-
mented self to others. Charlie, as Ted tells it, fared less well. "Old Tobin
run the hotel in Tupper Lake Junction. Charlie made up a song about
himself, and that Tobin's daughter come into it. Charlie fooled himself.
He went right into this Tobin's hotel, and somebody got him to sing. He
was pretty drunk, and he went over to Tobin and his daughter and sung
it":

THE ROVING CUNNINGHAM

I am that roving Cunningham, well, I roam from town to town;
Whenever I get a job to work, I'm willing to set down;
With my staff upon my shoulder, and my kit upon my hand,
And it's back to Saranac I will go, that roving Cunningham.

When I first came to Tupper Lake, the girls all jumped with joy,
Saying one unto the other, "Here comes that roving boy!"
While one treats me to the bottle, and another to a dram,
And the toasts went round the table: "Here's to that healthy young
    Cunningham."

Now, I hadn't been in Tupper Lake a day not more than three,
When Tobin's lovely daughter, she fell in love with me.
She said she wanted to marry me, and takes me by the hand,
And she slightly told her mother she loved young Cunningham.

It's "Hold your tongue, you silly fool! How dare you say so?
How could you love that little bum you never saw before?"
"Now, hold your tongue, dear mother, and it's do the best you can,
For back to Saranac I will go with that roving Cunningham."

"That there was pretty raw, for a lousy no-good bum to come right in
there and sing that. You know, they were quite important people. They
were people with money. The only child they had was that one daughter.
She was a beautiful girl. Jesus, it was all just something that he had
thought up. But old Tobin didn't like his thoughts, I guess! This Tobin
weighed probably 280. Tobin took him right by the seat of the pants, and
neck, and throwed him right slick and clean out over the porch and right
out onto the street! That's what he got for singing *that* one!"

Ted Ashlaw has spent many years thinking about Cunningham and
that mistake in judgment. Perhaps things could have been different for
Ted, too. Sitting at home, talking about his experience as an Adirondack
woods singer, he likes to think so. "In 1934, I got a little song off from
a record. It was a big hit," Ted remembers, in reference to Jimmie
Rodgers's "Moonlight and Skies" (Victor 23574, released in 1931).

If I sung that song once that summer, I sung it ten thousand times. Everyone
would say "Sing that song! Sing that song!"

We pulled in pretty drunk, coming from Vermont, into the Waverly Hotel
there to St. Regis Falls. They had me sing that song. And there was an old man
with big chin whiskers and a big German police dog on a leash. I sung that in
there, and he called me over.

Said, "How would you like to go with me? How much money do you make in the woods?"

I said, "It ain't much—$2.50 a day."

He said, "I can start you in with $100 a week, and I could have you making $1,000 a week in no time at all."

You know, if he hadn't been an old man, I'd have hit him. I thought he was making fun of me. That's what I thought. By Jesus, I come to find out he wasn't. He was a producer and it was all right—as I found out after. As I've often said, I think everybody in this world has a chance at one time or other. And I flubbed it. I think that happens often.

Getting up from his kitchen chair, Ted rubs his hip and moves to his stove. Pouring another cup of coffee, he turns and says to me, "But Christ, it's been so long since I've even felt good enough to try to sing." It's August, 1976, and we both know that a chapter of his life has closed. And yet, we will see each other again and talk more about the songs, the singers, and the woods work. We will talk, too, about the recording sessions in his kitchen and during visits to the nostalgic, wood-paneled camp I occupied at Sterling Pond. There is much to remember, and we are both served well by that opportunity.

Notes

My field recordings of Ted's singing led to production of an album released in 1976: Ted Ashlaw, *Adirondack Woods Singer* (Philo 1022). The LP may be obtained through record outlets or by writing directly to Philo Records, Inc., The Barn, North Ferrisburg, Vt. 05473.

Walter Gunnison, news reporter for Ted's hometown of Hermon, wrote a fine feature article on the singer for the *St. Lawrence Plaindealer* (Canton, N.Y.), April 13, 1977. My chapter title is taken from his story lead.

"Willie Was as Fine a Sailor" has been infrequently collected in Canada and the United States. The story type is in keeping with many English and Irish street ballads of the late eighteenth and early nineteenth centuries, although the eerie supernatural retribution suggests links with earlier songs and folktales. See H. Richard Hayward, *Ulster Songs and Ballads* (London: Duckworth, 1925), pp. 82–84; Maureen Jolliffe, *The Third Book of Irish Ballads* (Cork: Mercier Press, 1970), pp. 74–76; and Manny and Wilson, *Songs of Miramichi*, pp. 308–9. Recorded version: Ashlaw, *Adirondack Woods Singer*.

"Donny Dims of the Arrow," or "The Braes of Yarrow" (Child 214), is found, for example, in Edith Fowke, ed., *The Penguin Book of Canadian Folk Songs* (Baltimore: Penguin Books, 1973), pp. 178–79; Fowke, *Traditional Singers and Songs*, pp. 62–63; Cazden, *Catskill Songbook*, pp. 40–41, and "Songs of the

Catskills," #45. In some versions Sarah commits suicide. Norman Cazden, "The Story of a Catskill Ballad," *New York Folklore Quarterly*, 8 (1952), 245–66, provides an in-depth study of the text, as does James Reed, *The Border Ballads* (London: Athlone Press, 1973), pp. 143–48. For tune and text variants, see Bertrand Harris Bronson, *The Singing Tradition of Child's Popular Ballads* (Princeton, N.J.: Princeton University Press, 1976), pp. 380–83. Recorded version: *Child Ballads, II*, The Folksongs of Britain, Vol. 5 (Caedmon 1146), coll. and ed. Peter Kennedy and Alan Lomax.

"Mickey Brannigan's Pup" seems to have circulated among woodsmen mainly in eastern Ontario and the lumbering areas of New York State. See, for example, Cazden, "Songs of the Catskills," #122. The piece was printed in various Irish-American songsters, among them *Wehman Bros.' Pocket Size Irish Song Book, No. 1* (New York: Wehman Bros., 1909), p. 116. Recorded version: Ashlaw, *Adirondack Woods Singer*.

"Paddy Magrue" (Child 81) has had considerable currency in North America, although explicitly "dirty" versions (Ted's label) are rarely recorded or printed in folksong collections. See Renwick's discussion in Coffin, *British Traditional Ballad*, rev. ed., where he suggests that "it is the very combination of the sensational transgression and the equally sensational punishment which holds such strong attraction for our singers . . ." (p. 238). Bronson, *Singing Tradition*, notes that "this ballad is one of those quoted in Beaumont and Fletcher's *Knight of the Burning Pestle* (ca. 1611), and it was entered in the Stationers' Register in 1630" (p. 210). Ted's rendition is most closely related to texts and tunes collected in New Brunswick and the Canadian Maritimes. In addition to Bronson, pp. 214–15 (the text refers to "young Magrue"), note MacEdward Leach, *Folk Ballads and Songs of the Lower Labrador Coast*, National Museum of Canada, Bulletin No. 201, Anthropological Series No. 68 (Ottawa: National Museum of Canada, 1965), pp. 32–35; Manny and Wilson, *Songs of Miramichi*, pp. 204–5; and Maud Karpeles, ed., *Folk Songs from Newfoundland* (Hamden, Conn.: Archon Books, 1970), pp. 60–66.

"Two Sons of North Britain" (Laws J12) is one of the more infrequently collected folksongs in Ted's repertory. Observes W. Roy Mackenzie, *Ballads and Sea Songs from Nova Scotia* (Cambridge, Mass.: Harvard University Press, 1928), "It seems probable that all versions of the song to be found in the United States came from Scotland by way of Canada" (p. 323). For additional versions, see Rickaby, *Shanty-Boy*, pp. 185–87, and Leach, *Lower Labrador Coast*, pp. 110–11. Recorded version: Ashlaw, *Adirondack Woods Singer*.

For "Cole Younger" (Laws E3), note Ohrlin, *Hell-Bound Train*, pp. 142–43 and the biblio-discography, p. 271. A study of the ballad and its background is found in John Q. Anderson, "Another Texas Variant of 'Cole Younger,' Ballad of a Badman," *Western Folklore*, 31 (1972), 103–15.

"The Gentle Boy" appears in Elizabeth B. Greenleaf and Grace Mansfield, eds., *Ballads and Sea Songs of Newfoundland* (Cambridge, Mass.: Harvard University Press, 1933), pp. 224–25. Recorded version: Ashlaw, *Adirondack Woods Singer*.

"My Little Rambling Rose" was written and composed by Harold Freeman, copyrighted 1917 by Garton Brothers Music Publishers, Boston, Mass.

"Lasca" has been frequently printed as a recitation piece attributed to Frank

Desprez, ca. 1888; the original poem is longer and more sentimental than the reworked version Ted sings. See also Austin E. Fife and Alta S. Fife, *Ballads of the Great West* (Palo Alto, Calif.: American West Publishing Co., 1970), pp. 208–10. The ballad has not been previously reported from northeastern folksong tradition. Ted uses essentially the same tune for "Joe Bowers" (Laws B14).

"Mother Was a Lady (or, If Jack Were Only Here)" was written and composed by Edward B. Marks and Joseph W. Stern in 1896. The sheet music has been reprinted in many song folios, including Robert Fremont, *Favorite Songs of the Nineties* (New York: Dover Publications, 1973), pp. 208–11. Sigmund Spaeth, *Read 'em and Weep: The Songs You Forgot to Remember* (1926; rpt., New York: Da Capo Press, 1979), pp. 170–72, discusses the song's origin, noting that it was inspired by a waitress overheard in a New York City restaurant. Ted may have learned his version from a 1928 Jimmie Rodgers release (Victor 21433).

"Driving Saw-Logs on the Plover" (Laws dC29) refers to a tributary of the Wisconsin River; the ballad was composed by W. N. Allen ("Shan T. Boy") in 1873. Ted probably learned it from a 1928 commercial issue (Columbia 15278-D) featuring "Pierre La Dieu," a pseudonym for American popular singer Oscar Grogan. For additional versions from loggers, see Fowke, *Lumbering Songs from the Northern Woods*, pp. 204–5, and Rickaby, *Shanty-Boy*, pp. 89–91. Recorded version: Ashlaw, *Adirondack Woods Singer*.

"Miner Hill" and "Beaver River" are good examples of lumbercamp "moniker songs." Beck, *They Knew Paul Bunyan*, includes similar pieces and describes the popular format: "Moniker songs record in verse the personalities of real people. Sometimes they recount an event, sometimes they take the form of an ode. Often, if the poet had been impressed enough with the camp, he simply recorded the names of the shanty boys working there together, with short comments about their characters" (p. 215). The "derry down" tune was widely adopted. "Miner Hill" bears close resemblance to the central Adirondack lumbering ballad "Blue Mountain Lake" (Laws C20); texts are found in Cutting, *Lore of an Adirondack County*, p. 20, and Hochschild, *Lumberjacks and Rivermen*, p. 48. Recorded version: Ashlaw, *Adirondack Woods Singer*.

Charlie Cunningham's story about the cow and five calves is Tale Type 1567F, "Hungry Shepherd Attracts Attention," versions of which have been reported from Europe and New Mexico (Motif J1341.6). A text translated from Spanish appears in Dorson, *Buying the Wind*, pp. 445–46.

Background material on "A Hobo's Life" is found in Fowke, *Traditional Singers and Songs*, pp. 112–13 (text and tune for "The Faggot Cutter") and p. 187 (notes on the British source). Recorded versions: LaRena Clark, *A Canadian Garland: Folksongs from the Province of Ontario* (Topic 12T140), and Ashlaw, *Adirondack Woods Singer*.

Notes for "The Roving Ashlaw Man" apply also to "The Roving Cunningham."

8

Beyond Sunday Rock

It is time to return to Sunday Rock. Books of this nature are apt to conclude with a swan song on the passing of the old order and lore identified with it. The convention is attractive, but it misses the mark. In the absence of a recoverable past, one durable through human voices, this folklore study would have been quite different. In essence, it would have been archival "lore" minus living "folk."

Much of the treatment does in fact document echoes from the Adirondack woods. Mirroring my field experience, the book began with elderly men who tell stories anchored for the most part in the past. The men's talk is largely about times gone by, yarns recollected from former-day experience and learning. The people and events depicted in the accounts often come across as divorced, or at least distanced, from the present. Much like Sunday Rock, the stories are in one sense vestiges of an earlier day.

Yet to emphasize that element is to slight the carry-over of the past into the present. Sunday Rock and woodsmen's storytelling in the western foothills endure. Both remain meaningful because of shared experiences and emotional attachments. Together, rock and stories symbolize and promote durable associations of an interpersonal sort. Behind each of the voices, and implicit in each account, is the assumption that spoken words expressive of the native regional experience are worth sharing with others—strangers as well as friends. That is especially true when the words capture and convey something indelible about memorable persons, places, and situations.

The high value placed upon talk is by no means limited to men in the North Country. There are plenty of women "talkers" in the western foothills. From my observations, however, they appear less inclined than men to display talk about woods-based experience, particularly talk of an artistic sort, in woods or public barroom contexts. The same pattern seems to hold for domestic surroundings. I do not mean that women are less talkative. Rather, they are talkative about different matters and tend to stylize that talk primarily in those domestic and private settings where they are in the immediate company of other women.

But whatever the sex grouping or the occasion, appreciation of the spoken word brings people together in the foothills. Among adults, notably the elderly, interpersonal contact often results in "stopping to visit awhile." In the North Country (elsewhere, too) that activity implies more than a casual get-together. For the term "to visit" refers both to the encounter and to the informal discourse that takes place during it.

In its social component, visiting is a small-group phenomenon, often an in-group one. It binds people together, serving to define, reinforce, and extend relations. Among friends who have not seen one another for some time, visiting confirms and reaffirms old ties; among brief acquaintances or strangers, it is one way of establishing grounds on which to build a potential friendship. In my field research I often ran into situations where contacts made comments like "It's been nice to visit with you," or "I enjoyed visiting awhile with you." I was always struck by these remarks since it was I who had "paid the visit," not vice versa.

In its verbal component, visiting usually involves a mixture of information exchange, gossip, and what amounts to talk for the sake of talk. Among elderly woodsmen the content often fuses with reminiscence and storytelling entertainment. I credit Dave Snow of Madrid, a retired town highway department employee, with making clear to me in 1971 the full significance of that fusion:

> There used to be an old Bill Ashley up there to Hermon who used to tell some pretty good yarns. He made them up just like he was going along talking about a neighbor or something. He worked on the road there for years. And some of the older fellas ought to know better. They'd all get to the oil shack at noon here and tell the stories. And it'd take him a whole hour to tell one story. You'd think he was talking about his neighbor or something, the way he was telling it. Some of them afterwards would get on a job [and say], "You suppose that's so?" He'd never bat an eyelash—just as sober as can be.

The account helped me realize the importance of what Hep Hepburn had said a year earlier, that stories told in the woods "got embellished a little as they were told over and over." Visiting in its social and verbal components brings people and events to the fore. Yarns, in turn, celebrate memorable people and events, and often such stories are the direct product of artistically structured verbal "visiting." In short, I came to appreciate woodsmen's yarns as capsules of experience—time capsules, if you will, containing memorable images and impressions preserved in words. Clearly, elderly woodsmen in the foothills share that appreciation on both sides of Sunday Rock.

The songs of western Adirondack lumbermen also convey a sense of photographs-in-words, but ones more frayed nowadays than the narratives in oral prose. The song tradition flourished at a time when most foothills loggers worked on a series of cutting, hauling, and river-driving jobs. As the Ashlaw brothers and others moved from locale to locale, and camp to camp, male camaraderie became all-important. Together, the transience and networks of companionship meant that fixed gathering spots assumed special significance. Those contexts included area homes, lumbercamp bunkhouses, and public barrooms. Song performances, like storytelling, were an extension of self to others through the medium of entertainment.

Industry change and the demise of sleep-in lumbercamps did not, in themselves, undermine the currency of the song heritage. Rather, the occupational transition contributed to a trend already underway by the 1940s in homes and barrooms. Then, as today, commercially recorded singers and songs were as accessible as the nearest phonograph, radio, or jukebox. Country-western counterparts superseded ballads and lyrics of a nonlumbering variety. The outmoded songs, along with esoteric lumbering material, slipped into the recesses of memory. And it is in memory that these songs, more than the tales, remain lodged. "Every once in a while now," says Eddie Ashlaw, "you'll ride along and one will come back to me that I haven't thought of in years."

As yet there has been no appreciable folksong revival among former loggers or their descendants in Northern New York. Revitalization of interest in the grassroots song heritage of the western foothills may someday come, as it has recently for old-time fiddling. But formal folk music concerts, staged contests, and foot-stomping festivals attracting large numbers of strangers and young people are alien, ultimately, to the men and traditions I write about. As Ted Ashlaw once put it, "I don't think I'd fit in with that type of crowd." While typical of Ted, the feeling seems widely shared among the woodsmen I came to know. They have many pleasant memories of song- and tale-swapping beyond Sunday Rock. Perhaps that is enough.

Notes

My summing up builds upon Richard Bauman, "The La Have Island General Store: Sociability and Verbal Art in a Nova Scotia Community," *Journal of American Folklore*, 85 (1972), 330–41. Also helpful was J. A. Barnes, *Social Networks*, Addison-Wesley Module in Anthropology, 26 (Reading, Mass.: Addison-Wesley Publishing Co., 1972).

For details of the fiddling heritage in St. Lawrence County, see my article "Old-Time Fiddling and Social Dance in Central St. Lawrence County," *New York Folklore Quarterly*, 30 (1974), 163–82, reprinted with revisions and photographs in the St. Lawrence County Historical Association *Quarterly*, 23 : 1 (Jan., 1978), 15–19.

Index

Acuff, Roy, 121
Adirondack Museum, 10*n*, 24*n*
Adirondack Park, 13
Adirondacks. *See* Northern New York
"After the Ball," 58
"Ain't I Crazy," 57
Alcohol: and logger "blowouts," 32, 63;
　and storytelling, 42, 44, 47, 50, 132;
　and singing, 58, 80, 89, 90, 94, 108–9,
　131–34; in lumbercamps, 63, 108–9,
　132
"Allen Bayne," 102
Anecdotes: as story type, 29, 31, 47, 48,
　50; examples of, 29–32, 48–50
Anguinum, 17
Arnold, Jack, 66
Arnold, Sam, 66
A. Sherman Lumber Company, 66
Ashlaw, Eddie: as logger, 14, 18, 23, 31,
　82–83, 129; as river-driver, 18, 31; as
　singer, 61, 68, 74–75, 80, 84–90, 101,
　131, 141; and social drinking, 80, 81,
　83, 91; and relationship between drink
　and song, 80, 89–90, 94, 97; biography
　of, 82–84, 96; life philosophy of, 84,
　94, 96; aesthetic of, as singer, 88; as
　songmaker, 91–97, 98*n*
Ashlaw, Levi, 82
Ashlaw, Ted: biography of, 14, 99–101,
　135–36; as logger, 15, 18–19, 94, 99,
　100; as river-driver, 18–19; as story-
　teller, 27, 29, 33; as singer, 58, 61, 64,
　99, 101–36; singing style of, 64, 103,
　121, 124–25; aesthetic of, as singer, 66,
　122–25 *passim*; as songmaker, 125,

127–31; compared with brother Eddie,
　99, 101, 131
Ashley, Bill, 140
"At a Kind Old Mother's Side," 102
Averill, Harv, 4

Bacheller, Irving, 57
"Bad Companions," 57
"The Bad Girl's Lament," 102
Bagpipes, 57
Bangor, Maine, 12
Banjos, 64
"The Banks of Little Eau Pleine," 102
"Barbara Allen," 102, 109
Barrooms: storytelling in, ix, x, 4, 41–52;
　singing in, x, 55, 58, 64, 68, 74–75, 80,
　89, 96, 101, 108, 112, 132; logger
　"blowouts" in, 30, 63, 83
"The Basket Maker's Child," 57
"The Basket of Eggs," 102
"The Battle of Fredericksburg." *See* "Just
　before the Last Great Fight"
Bay Pond, 82
Bears: stories about, 28–29, 36*n*, 51, 53*n*,
　54*n*
Beaver River, 66, 82, 92, 94, 127, 131, 132
"Beaver River," 102, 127–31, 138*n*
Bedbugs: stories about, 16, 24*n*, 41
Berry, Charlie, 3, 7
Big Bertha, 51–52, 54*n*
Big stories. *See* Lies
Big Woods. *See* Woods
Binan, Arthur, 126
Binan, Lawrence, 127
Black flies: stories about, 41

143

"The Blind Child," 102
"Blue Mountain Lake," 138n
"The Bonneshai River," 58
"The Boston Burglar," 67
"The Braes of Yarrow." See "Donny Dims of the Arrow"
Brandreth, N.Y., 82
Brooklyn Cooperage Company, 3, 30
Brothall, Paul, 32
Brown, Harlan, 32
Brown, Hayden (Hadie): epithets used by, 11, 32–33; stories about, 30–33, 36n, 46; as storyteller, 32, 33
Bruce, Jack, 29
Bulls: stories about, 31
Bunkhouses: life in, 15–16; storytelling in, 26–29; singing in, 61, 74, 108–9
Bunyan, Paul, 33–35, 36n, 37n
"Bush LaPorte." See "I'm Just a Common Lumberhick"
Butler, Deacon, 4

Camps, 4, 6, 42
Canton, N.Y., 34, 58
Carter Family, 109
"Casey Was Dancing with a Strawberry Blond," 58
Cassel, Fred, 38–40
Cazden, Norman, 76n, 137n
Cedar Lodge, 4, 41, 42
Celoon, Pete, 107
Center for the Study of North Country Folklife, 10n
Childwold, N.Y., 16, 82, 96
Chisholm, Big, 30
Clark, Bill, 17
Clark, Mrs. Simeon, 11
Clement, Joe, 27
Clergy: in stories, 27, 36n; in lumber-camps, 61
Cleveland, Sara, 77n
Coaxing: singing and, 58, 61, 89
"Cold Harbor 1864," 57
"Cole Younger," 102, 113, 114–16, 137n
Colton, N.Y., 3, 10n, 17, 29, 42, 67
"The Colton Boy," 67
Corbett, Bill, 45–52 passim
"Cottage by the Sea," 102
"Cousin Nellie," 61–63, 77n, 78n, 102
Cowboy songs. See Western songs
Cows: stories about, 132, 138n
Cranberry Lake, N.Y., 63
Creighton, Thomas, 91–95 passim

"The Cruel Ship's Carpenter," 55
Cunningham, Charlie: as singer, 108, 112, 131–35; as songmaker, 132–35
Cutting, Edith E., 10n, 76n

Dancing, 60, 61
Daniel, Mat, 4
Daniels, Frank, 27–33 passim, 56–57, 63
Daniels, Tess, 57
Davignon, John, 129
Declamando ending: in traditional singing, 125
Deer: stories about, 4, 6, 33, 41–42, 46, 47, 50, 53n; euphemisms for, 38
DeLong, Guy, 32, 63
Denny, Dave, 123
Dirty songs. See Obscene songs
Dogs: stories about, 28–29, 47, 53n
Domestic singing: and woods singing tradition, 57–58, 61, 84, 101, 107, 108
"Donny Dims of the Arrow," 102, 105–7, 136n, 137n
"Don't Say Goodbye If You Must Go," 89
"Don't Send My Boy to Prison," 102
"Down by the Sea Shore," 102
Downey, Bill, 31
Downey and Snell, 30
Draper Corporation, 100
Drinking. See Alcohol
"Driving Saw-Logs on the Plover," 102, 123–24, 138n
"The Drummer Boy's Burial," 57
"The Drunkard's Doom," 58
Ducks: stories about, 47
Duffy, Fay, 11, 31–32
"The Dying Soldier," 67, 102

Evergreen Hotel, 63, 74

F. A. Cutting and Son, 30, 126
"The Faggot Cutter." See "A Hobo's Life"
Family Herald, 57, 77n
Farmer, Arthur, 27
"The Farmer's Curst Wife," 102
Fayette, Levi, 126
Ferry, Hamilton (Ham): as storyteller, 16–17, 30, 41–52; as guide, 42, 44, 48–50; biography of, 43–44; as singer, 66, 68, 70–73, 80; memory of, 68–70; aesthetic of, as singer, 72
Fiddling, 57, 58, 91, 92, 94, 141, 142n
Fieldwork: author's goals of, ix, x, xi, 3, 44, 76n, 139; author's method in, ix, x,

44–45, 51, 52, 75, 80, 89, 90–91, 109,
    112, 119, 136, 140
"Fifteen Years Ago Today," 102
Fishing: stories about, 4, 27, 41, 42,
    51–52
"Floyd Collins," 57
"The *Flying Cloud*," 57
Folksongs: collections of, described, x,
    76*n*, 77*n*
Foremen: stories about, 29–33, 60–61
Fort Jackson, N.Y., 126
Fowke, Edith, 76*n*, 91
Francis, Junior, 89
Franklin Co., 14
French-Canadians: in St. Lawrence Co., 7,
    58, 82; as loggers, 12, 18, 92, 94; in sto-
    ries, 26, 29–30, 36*n*, 38–40; as singers,
    58; in songs, 92, 94, 130
Frizzell, Lefty, 121

"The Gay Spanish Maid," 102
Geese: stories about, 48–50, 53*n*
"The Gentle Boy," 102, 116, 117, 137*n*
Glens Falls, N.Y., 12
"The Goddamn Wheel," 102
"Good-bye, Jenny Jones," 102
"Good Old Dollar Bill," 102
"Gospel of Treasure," 102, 112
Gould Paper Company, 82
"Grace Brown and Chester Gillette," 67
Grand Union Hotel, 63, 74, 83
Grant, Roll, 66
Grass River, 19
Grogan, Oscar, 138*n*
Guides: stories about, 6, 38–40, 41,
    47–48
Guiney, Jim, 25
Gunnison, Walter, 136*n*
Guthrie, Claude, 58–61
Guthrie, George, 58–61

Haines, Howard, 129, 130, 131
Ham's Inn, 41–43, 63, 74, 80
Harmonicas, 57, 60, 61
Hayes, Jerry, 91, 93, 95, 96
Hepburn, Lionel (Hep), 29–30, 140
Herkimer Co., 82
Hermon, N.Y., 14, 99, 140
Hickey, Jim, 68
"A Hobo's Life," 102, 132, 133–34, 138*n*
Hogansburg, N.Y., 25
Hollywood, N.Y., 66, 83
Hollywood Club, 41

Hopkinton, N.Y., 30, 82, 103
Hudson River, 12
Hunters, xi, 4, 9, 28–29, 38, 41–42,
    45–51
Hunting: stories about, 4, 6, 28–29, 33,
    41–42, 46–51
Hurley, Steve, 89

"I Had a Little Girl," 102
"I Know What It Means to Be Lonely,"
    102, 112
"I'm Just a Common Lumberhick," 91–
    96, 98*n*
"The Indian Maid." *See* "Lasca"
Indian River, 82
Indians, 25, 93
Inkslinger, Johnny, 34
Insects. *See* Black flies; Mosquitoes
Instrumental music: imitated, using mouth,
    57; in barrooms, 64
International Paper Company, 82
"In the Baggage Coach Ahead," 57, 58
Irish: in St. Lawrence Co., 7; as river-driv-
    ers, 18, 19; as singers, 77*n*, 103, 107
"The Irish Mail Robber," 102
Ives, Edward D., 76*n*, 77*n*

"Jack and Joe," 102
"Jack and the Chambermaid," 102
"Jack Haggerty," 72–73, 79*n*
"The Jam on Gerry's Rock," 55, 57,
    64–66, 67, 72, 78*n*, 89, 102, 125
Jerseyfield, N.Y., 83
Jew's harp, 57
"Jimmy's Mother Went to See Her Son,"
    102
"Joe Bowers," 102, 116, 138*n*
Joe Indian Pond, 30, 32
Jones, Elmer, 93, 123
Jordan River, 41, 66–67
Jukeboxes, 55, 74, 75, 141
"Just before the Last Great Fight," 102,
    112

Kade, Fred, 29–30
"Katie Morey," 102
Keith, Herbert F., 7, 10*n*
Killen, Johnny, 84
"Kisses Don't Lie," 102

"The Lake of Shilin," 58
Lake Ozonia, 30, 58, 66, 82, 125
LaPorte, Arthur (Bush), 16, 91, 94

"Lasca," 102, 119–21, 137*n*, 138*n*
Leaf, Peter (Pete), 25
Learning songs, 56, 68–74 *passim*, 84, 86, 91, 99, 101–8 *passim*, 112, 123
"The Letter Edged in Black," 57
Lewis Co., 82
Lice: stories about, 16–17, 24*n*, 41
Lies: as story type, discussed, 17, 27, 33–52 *passim*, 53*n*, 54*n*; examples of, 17, 27–52 *passim*
"Life's Railway to Heaven," 57
Limekiln Lake, 82, 94
Linn tractor, 21
Little Blue Mountain, 16, 17
"The Little Brown Cot," 57
"The Little Mohea," 102
"Little Musgrave and Lady Barnard." *See* "Paddy Magrue"
"The Little Rosewood Casket," 102
Lloyd Pond, 34
Long, Ned, 19–21, 31, 32
Long Pond, 96
Loon Lake, 82
Lucas, Sumner, 30, 33
Lumber Camp News, 24*n*, 74, 83
Lumbercamps: demise of, 11, 21, 23, 141; described, 14–16, 23; food in, 15, 38; storytelling in, 25–35 *passim*, 36*n*; singing in, 57, 61, 77*n*, 107, 108, 132
Lumbering: and storytelling, ix, x, 9, 11, 12, 16–17, 25–35, 36*n*, 132, 141; and singing, x, 55–138, 141; in Northern New York, 11, 12–13, 23, 24*n*; equipment and techniques of, 11–15, 18–21, 23; stories about, 11, 16–17, 24*n*, 25–35, 36*n*; and industry change, 11, 21, 23, 141; labor force, 13–14, 18, 23, 63, 83, 126–27, 129–30; pulpwood, 13, 15, 18–19, 23, 82, 83; work cycle in, 13–15, 18–21, 23, 63; hardwood, 15, 21, 83; wages, 15, 63, 91, 93, 94, 127, 136; songs about, 55, 58, 59–60, 64–66, 68, 76*n*, 84–86, 91–96, 123–24, 125–31
"The Lumberjack's Alphabet," 59–60, 77*n*

MacAleese, Cole, 74
McCarthy, Leo, 15, 16, 29
McGhee, Herb, 14
McGill, George, 27–29
McKeever, N.Y., 14
Madrid, N.Y., 140

Maldrin, Jock, 4
Mann, Art, 6
"Mantle So Green," 102
"The Mariner's Dream," 57
Massena, N.Y., 5
"May I Sleep in Your Barn Tonight, Mister?," 57
"May the Grass Grow Green above You," 57
Memory: and storytelling repertoire, 3–4, 9, 11, 23, 27, 35, 141; and song repertoire, 68–74 *passim*, 96, 101, 108, 141
"Message from over the Sea," 102
"Mickey Brannigan's Pup," 102, 107–8, 125, 137*n*
"Miner Hill," 102, 125–27, 138*n*
Monica, Wilfred, 64, 84, 94, 103, 112, 117
Moniker songs: described, 138*n*. *See also* Songmaking
Moody, Mart, 47–48, 50–51, 52*n*
"Moonlight and Skies," 102, 135
Moose: stories about, 38–40, 53*n*
Moosehead Stillwater, 4
Moose River, 18, 82
Mosquitoes: stories about, 41, 53*n*
"Mother Was a Lady (or, If Jack Were Only Here)," 102, 121–22, 138*n*
Mouth organs. *See* Harmonicas
"My Little Rambling Rose," 102, 117, 118–19, 137*n*
"My Mother-in-Law Was Sick One Day," 102

Newton Brothers, 16
Nicholville, N.Y., 89
"Noble Lads of Canada," 57
"Nobody Cares for the Poor," 57
North Country. *See* Northern New York
Northern New York: as locale, ix, x, 7; folklore collecting in, x, 10*n*, 76*n*, 77*n*; as folksong area, x, 67, 76*n*, 77*n*, 103
Norwood, N.Y., 64
Numskulls: stories about, 26–27, 35*n*, 36*n*

Obscene songs: woods singers and, 56, 61–63, 137*n*; clergy and, 61; children and, 61; women and, 61, 62, 63
"Oh Dem Golden Slippers," 57
"Oh No, My Boy, Not I," 102
Older, Lawrence, 77*n*
"The Old Front Door," 57

"An Old Gray Ghost Hitched at a Post," 58
Olsen, Ole, 35
"Only an Old Song," 57
Oral history: mentioned, 4, 9, 12
Oswegatchie River, 12
Oval Wood Dish Company, 3, 82, 91, 93, 94, 95

"Paddy Magrue," 102, 109–11, 137n
Paradise, Harry, 129–31 passim
Parishville, N.Y., 4, 11, 14, 28, 30, 56, 63, 90
Parishville Center, N.Y., 80, 90
Parker, Benjamin S., 57
"The Patchwork Quilt," 57
"Peggy Gordon," 102
Pelow, Johnny, 84, 103, 105, 107, 112, 125
"The Perfect Moose Caller," 38–40
Photographs: songs as, 9, 70, 141; stories as, 9, 141; used in storytelling, 46, 47
"A Picture from Life's Other Side," 102, 112
Piercefield, N.Y., 15
Planty, Myron, 126
Pleasant Mound Cemetery, 3
Poetry: recitations of, 54n; and song repertoire, 57, 70, 74
Poles, 33, 130
"Poor Little Joe," 102
Porter, Marjorie Lansing, 77n
Potsdam, N.Y., 3, 5, 12, 21, 48, 66, 89
Pruff, Joe, 83

Radios: in lumbercamps, 57, 74, 79n, 141; and song repertoire, 58, 74, 86, 109, 112, 123, 125, 141
Raquette Lake, 16
Raquette River, 3, 10n, 12, 19, 31, 44, 66, 68, 72, 83
Raquette River Paper Company, 21
Recitations, 54n, 67, 74
Records: influence of, on song tradition, 55, 56, 74, 86, 89, 109, 112, 121, 123, 125, 135, 138n, 141
"The Red-Light Saloon," 102
Red River, 82
Regan, John, 67
Reputation: of storytellers, 4, 25–33 passim, 42–43, 47–48, 52; of singers, 60, 80, 101
"The Rich Merchant," 103

River-drivers, 15, 18–20, 31, 32, 38, 44, 60–68 passim
River-driving: food and, 18; described, 18–19, 31, 60–68 passim, 84–86; songs about, 64–66, 68, 72–73, 78n, 79n, 84–86, 97n, 98n, 123–24, 138n
Road monkeys, 11
Rodgers, Jimmie, 135, 138n
" 'Root Hog or Die' Is Hitler's Battle Cry," 103
"The Roving Ashlaw Man," 97, 98n, 134
"The Roving Cunningham," 103, 134–35, 138n

"The Sailor's Alphabet," 57, 59
St. Lawrence Co.: geography of, ix, 3, 7; folklife study in, ix–x, 10n; population of, 7; economy of, 7; history of, 7, 9, 10n; map, 8
St. Lawrence Plaindealer, 136n
St. Lawrence River, 12
St. Louis, Avery, 34–35
St. Regis Falls, N.Y., 26, 82, 135
St. Regis Paper Company, 3, 14, 19, 29, 82, 94
St. Regis River, 63
"Sam Bass," 57
Santa Clara, N.Y., 14
Saranac Lake, N.Y., 30, 99, 131, 135
"Satisfied Mind," 103
Schofell, Otis, 3–4, 7, 31, 66
Service, Robert W., 54n
Sevey, N.Y., 4, 74
Sevey's Hotel, 51, 63, 64
Singing style, 55, 58, 64, 74, 77n, 88, 103, 121, 124–25
Sisson and White, 82, 91, 93, 96
S. L. Clark and Son Company, 11
Smith, Carl, 121
Smith, Harry, 129, 130
Snow, Dave, 140
Sochia, Elroy, 4, 5, 23, 42
Songmaking: local and topical, 66–68, 91–96, 125–35, 138n; scholarship on, 76n
South Colton, N.Y., 7, 19, 21, 25, 31
Spear, Glenn, 4–6, 33
Spears, Jimmy, 60–61
Stark, N.Y., 31
Sterling Pond, 35, 90, 136
"Stick to Your Mother, Tom," 57
Stillwater Reservoir, 94
Stockholm, N.Y., 63

Storytelling style, 28, 38–39, 48, 50, 52, 53n, 140
"The Stowaway Boy," 103
Stowe, Harold (Bub), 21, 25–27, 33
Sullivan, James (Jim), 91, 93, 95, 96
"Sunbeam in the Sky," 103
Sunday Rock, 7, 9, 10n, 139
Sunday Rock Association, 7
Supernault, George, 127
Swedes, 30

Tall tales. See Lies
"Tebo," 66, 67, 78n
"The Tenderfoot," 86–88, 89, 96, 98n, 103
Thibault, Joe, 67. See also "Tebo"
Thomas, Howard, 10n
Thompson, Harold W., 10n, 76n
Timber Tavern, 90
Tourists, ix, 9, 42, 51–52, 141
"The Trail to Mexico," 103
Tubb, Ernest, 112
Tupper Lake, N.Y., 3, 13, 19, 63, 74, 75, 82, 83, 94, 95, 96, 99, 132, 135
Tupper Lake Junction, N.Y., 63, 83
"'Twas Only an Irishman's Dream," 103
"Twenty-one Years," 57
"Two Sons of North Britain," 103, 113–14, 137n
Tyler, Helen Escha, 10n

Usher Farm, 96
"Utah Carl," 70–72, 78n

Visiting: described, 140; and storytelling, 140–41, 142n; and singing, 141

Waverly Hotel, 135

Weather: stories about, 17, 33, 51
Western songs, 70–72, 74, 78n, 86, 98n, 114–16, 119–21, 137n, 138n
"When the Work's All Done This Fall," 57, 103
"Where the Silvery Colorado Wends Its Way," 57
"Whispering Bill," 57
Wick, N.Y., 30, 33
"The Wild Colonial Boy," 67, 103, 125
"The Wild Mustard River," 84–86, 90, 97n, 103
"Willie Was as Fine a Sailor," 103–5, 112, 136n
Willis, Uncle Eben, 4
Wolf Pond, 29
Women: in lumber woods, 13; and talk, 38, 42, 139–40
Woods, George, 27
Woods: as male domain, x, 7, 9, 38, 40–41, 140–41
Woods Lake, 82
Woodsmen: as group, ix, 7, 9, 38, 141
Woods singers: as group, x, 55, 56, 61, 99, 125; song repertoires of, 55–56, 57, 58, 67, 68, 70, 72, 74, 76n, 84, 86, 90, 99, 101, 102–3, 108, 112–24; and audiences, 64, 74, 89, 96, 108–9, 134. See also Songmaking
Worms: stories about, 51–52, 54n
Writing: as aid in learning songs, 70, 101, 108; in song composing, 93, 125, 127

Yankee: stereotype of, ix
"You'll Never Know a Mother's Love Again," 57
"Young Charlotte," 67
"The Young Irish Boy," 103